Teaching Middle School Mathematics
Activities, Materials, and Problems

Stephen Krulik

Jesse A. Rudnick

Temple University

Allyn and Bacon
Boston   London   Toronto   Sydney   Tokyo   Singapore

Series editor: *Norris Harrell*
Series editorial assistant: *Bridget Keane*
Marketing managers: *Ellen Dolberg/ Brad Parkins*
Manufacturing buyer: *Suzanne Lareau*

Copyright © 2000 by Allyn & Bacon
A Pearson Education Company
Needham Heights, MA 02494

Internet: www.abacon.com

Library of Congress Cataloging-in-Publication Data

Krulik, Stephen.
    Teaching middle school mathematics : activities, materials, and
problems / Stephen Krulik, Jesse A. Rudnick.
      p.   cm.
    Includes index.
    ISBN 0-205-28628-3
    1. Mathematics--Study and teaching (Middle school) I. Rudnick,
Jesse A. II. Title.
    QA11 .K818 1999
    510'.71'273--dc21   99-19375
                                           CIP

Printed in the United States of America
10 9 8 7 6 5 4 3 2 1   03 02 01 00 99

CONTENTS

PREFACE

School mathematics is currently in the midst of a new revolution—a revolution that has identified reasoning, problem solving, and communication skills as major objectives. This is partly due to the efforts of the National Council of Teachers of Mathematics and the publication of their three-volume *Standards*, but also in response to the demands being placed on educators by the emergence of new kinds of technology. The current curriculum has placed problem solving, reasoning, and communication skills on a par with the traditional computational and algorithmic skills. In addition, the curriculum has been expanded to include topics previously reserved for higher grade levels; for instance, we find topics in geometry, statistics, algebra, as well as probability and statistics permeating the elementary and middle school programs.

These new areas of study are placing increased demands on teachers' time. Teachers must learn how to help children attain facility in problem solving and reasoning. At the same time, they are required to teach their students these new concepts as well as the basic computational and algorithmic skills. This added emphasis has had the greatest impact on teaching mathematics in the middle grades. In many cases, these new topics include mathematics that teachers may never have encountered before, and, as a result, have not as yet developed the pedagogical strategies needed.

Teachers feel more comfortable and are more effective if they have a resource of ideas and materials that they can use to expand and enhance their day-to-day teaching of mathematics. All teachers are constantly looking for activities to motivate and help their students maintain and improve their skills and to increase their mathematical power. This book contains a variety of activities, aids, and materials that will satisfy this need. It also includes materials that teachers can use to help their students develop better reasoning and problem-solving skills. In addition, problem-solving activities will be included throughout the book, applied to the topic at hand.

HOW TO USE THIS BOOK

Teaching Middle School Mathematics is a collection of activities, aids, games, materials, and problems to help you in your mathematics classroom. Each activity provides you with the basis for an innovative, hands-on lesson to develop a mathematical concept, reinforce a skill, and gain experience in problem solving and reasoning. The activities include mathematical topics such as whole numbers, fractions, decimals, percents, geometry, algebra, and probability and statistics. Each activity will be presented with a common format, as follows:

Title: Each activity will be given a title or name.

Purpose and Topic: The purpose of the activity and the mathematical topic covered will be stated.

Materials: When appropriate, the materials required for this activity will be listed. In some cases, the Reproduction Pages in the back of the book will provide the necessary materials.

How to Make It: Directions will be provided on how to make the aid, game, or device.

How to Use It: Directions for implementing the activity will be presented. When appropriate, key questions and points of discussion will be suggested.

Extensions: In some cases, suggestions will be given for modifying or expanding the activity in order to cover additional mathematics topics or to provide additional practice.

Problems: Problem-solving experiences related to the topic will accompany many of the activities.

Teacher's Notes: Space will often be provided at the end of an activity in which you can record interesting questions that arose during the implementation of the activity or that you want to be certain to include the next time. You may also find some notes to consider when you implement the activity with your students.

Reproduction pages, black line masters, and activity materials will also be provided when appropriate. To use this book successfully, look up in the index the topic you are planning to teach. Examine the suggested activities and select those that are most appropriate for your needs. Feel free to modify an activity to suit the grade level and abilities of your students.

ACKNOWLEDGMENTS

Our appreciation goes to the following reviewers for their comments on the manuscript: Doug Brumbaugh, University of Central Florida; Nicholas A. Holodick, King's College; Karen Lafferty, Morehead State University; and Irwin Ozer, Richardson ISD.

Also by Stephen Krulik and Jesse A. Rudnick

The New Sourcebook for Teaching Reasoning and Problem Solving in Junior and Senior High School
ISBN: 0-205-16520-6

The New Sourcebook for Teaching Reasoning and Problem Solving in Elementary School
ISBN: 0-205-14826-3

Reasoning and Problem Solving: A Handbook for Elementary School Teachers
ISBN: 0-205-14006-8

Assessing Reasoning and Problem Solving: A Sourcebook for Elementary School Teachers
ISBN: 0-205-19854-6

For more information or to purchase a book, please call 1-800-278-3525.

CHAPTER ONE

Whole Numbers

ACTIVITY 1

Title: "Target 500"

Purpose and Topic: This activity provides students with extensive practice in addition of whole numbers. It also encourages the use of logic to adjust the numbers chosen, in order to get closer to the target score of 500.

Materials: Reproduction Page 1

How to Use It: Give each student a copy of Reproduction Page 1. Each student then selects four numbers and places one in each corner position of the outside square in the array. Now fill in the blank circles on each side by adding the two numbers in the circles on the vertices of that side. These sums become the vertices of the next square. Repeat this process until the "Target" position is reached. The object of the game is to come as close to 500 as possible.

A display board can be provided in the classroom for students to post their results and see who can reach exactly 500. The following figure shows a "Target" result of 504 as an example.

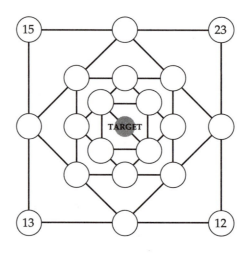

Extensions: This activity can be extended in the following ways:

(a) Try "Magic Squares" as a modification of "Target 500." A magic square is a square array in which the sums of the numbers in each row, column, and diagonal are the same. Present the students with a copy of Reproduction Page 2, which looks like this:

		6
	5	
4		2

Ask the students to complete the magic square. (The results are shown here.)

8	1	6
3	5	7
4	9	2

(b) As a further extension, have the students create their own 3 × 3 magic square using the numbers 9 through 17. An interesting method for solving any 3 × 3 magic square is as follows. First, find the sum of the nine numbers being used. In this case, $9 + 10 + 11 + 12 + 13 + 14 + 15 + 16 + 17 = 117$. Divide by 3. This is the "magic sum" (in this case, 39). Now, using these numbers, list all triples whose sum is 39:

9-13-17	10-12-17	11-12-16	12-13-14
9-14-16	10-13-16	11-13-15	
	10-14-15		

The center cell of the magic square is used four times. The only number to appear four times in the eight sets of triples is 13. Therefore, place 13 in the center cell. Next, consider the corner cells. These are each used in three sums (horizontally, vertically, and diagonally). Place 10-12-14-16 in the four corners, being certain the diagonal sums are each 39. Now complete the magic square. One possible result is shown here:

10	15	14
17	13	9
12	11	16

A creative student may recognize that adding 8 to each cell of the original magic square will produce the correct answer.

Problem: Jan hit the following dart board with 4 darts. She scored 61. How might she have done this?

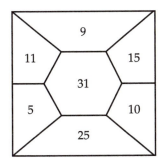

Discussion: There are multiple answers to this problem, solved by guess and test. Some possibilities include $31 + 10 + 10 + 10$, $15 + 10 + 11 + 25$, $31 + 9 + 11 + 10$, and so on.

An interesting situation arises by removing the 10 from the dart board and asking the same question. It is now impossible to score 61 with 4 darts, since all the numbers are now odd numbers, and the sum of four odd numbers will always be an even number.

Teacher's Notes:

ACTIVITY 2   **Title:** "Multiples of Three"

Purpose and Topic: This game setting provides students with the opportunity to practice addition of single-digit numbers while forming multiples of 3.

Materials: A 10" × 10" game board made from poster-board or oak-tag; 90 small 1" × 1" cards

How to Make It: Write the numerals from 1 through 9 on each of 10 small cards (10 of each digit). Divide the game board into 100 small 1" × 1" squares.

How to Use It: This game, which can be played by three or four students, is similar to Scrabble. The objective is to form number "strings" with the sum of its digits a multiple of 3.

Spread out the 90 small cards face down in the center of the group. Each player begins by taking 5 small cards. Play begins with the first player placing any number of his or her cards in any row or column on the board so that the sum of the numerals in the string is a multiple of 3. The player's score for that turn is the sum of the numerals in the line made. The player replaces the number of cards used by taking them from the pack in the center. (Each player must always have 5 cards in his or her hand until the replacement deck is exhausted.) Play continues by having each player in turn place from 1 through 5 cards in a row or column. A player must use at least one card already on the board in forming his or her line. Designate one player in the group to check on correct play and score. The winner is the player with the most points when play can no longer continue, or when some predesignated score has been reached. Here is the beginning of a typical game:

Player #1: 3, 1, 4, 7
Score: 15
Player #2: (1) 8, 9
Score: 18
Player #3: (8), 2, 2, 3
Score: 30

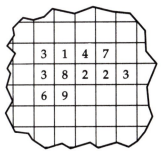

(Notice that Player #3 receives not only the line of numbers added but also the other numbers affected as well. Thus, the score here is 8 + 2 + 2 + 3 (= 15) and 4 + 2 + 7 + 2 (= 15) for a total of 30.)

Player #4: (3) 3, 6
Score: 45

Extensions: The game can easily be modified by requiring that the sum of each string's digits is a multiple of 4. Another possibility is that the sum of the numerals of the string must be a prime number.

Problem: The first three digits of a 5-digit number are 3, 4, and 6. Thus, the number can be represented as 34,6 _ _. What numerals would you place in the blanks so that the number would be

      (a) divisible by 3?   (b) divisible by 4?   (c) divisible by 5?
      (d) divisible by 6?

Discussion:

    (a) For a number to be divisible by 3, the sum of its digits must be divisible by 3.
    (b) For a number to be divisible by 4, the number formed by the final two digits must be divisible by 4.
    (c) For a number to be divisible by 5, the final digit must be a 5 or a 0.
    (d) For a number to be divisible by 6, it must be even and divisible by 3.

Teacher's Notes:

ACTIVITY 3   **Title:** "Let's Make a Number"

Purpose and Topic: This activity is a number game that provides students with an opportunity to practice simple addition. It also offers a chance for students to discover a "secret" that is based on an understanding of the base 10 number system.

Materials: None

How to Use It: Follow these simple steps:

(a) Have four students come to the board. Each is to write a 3-digit number, one under the other. For example, suppose these were the four numbers written by the students:

    287
    584
    161
    203

(b) Select any one of the four numbers and add 2997 to it. Write this new number on the board near the column of numbers that the students have written. Suppose you select 584 as the number. You would write 3581 on the chalkboard. (This will be the sum obtained when the game is completed.)

(c) Now add three numbers of your own to the four already written. Select your three numbers such that they represent the difference between each of the student's remaining numbers and 999. Do not add a number for the one already selected. Thus, for the four numbers previously shown, you would add 712 (999 – 287), 838 (999 – 161), and 796 (999 – 203).

(d) Ask another student to come to the board and find the sum of the seven numbers written there. This should be the sum you already wrote on the board at the beginning of the activity. Thus, this set of numbers would look like this:

    287
    584
    161
    203
    712
    838
    796
    ————
    3581

The sum of these numbers is the same as the sum previously written on the board.

Extensions: Try these modifications:

(a) Use 2-, 4-, or 5-digit numbers and repeat the game.

(b) Another possibility is to select a 5-digit number whose first digit is 2, and write it on the chalkboard. Now select a student from the class and tell him or her that the two of you are going to place five 4-digit numbers on the board, and the sum of the five numbers will be the number already written on the board. You begin by removing the first "2" and adding it to the remaining 4-digit number. Now, have the student write a 4-digit number under your number. You then write a 4-digit number that is the difference between the student's number and 9999. Say, for example, that you begin by selecting 26421 as your 5-digit number. Remove the first 2 and add it to 6421, giving you 6423.

You write:	6423
Student writes:	2135
You write:	7864
Student writes:	1234
You write:	8765

You now draw a line under these five numbers and add. The sum will be 26,421, as predicted.

Teacher's Notes:

ACTIVITY 4   **Title:** "Target 0"

Purpose and Topic: This activity provides students with extensive practice in subtraction of whole numbers. It also encourages the use of logic to adjust the numbers chosen, in order to get closer to the target score of 0.

Materials: Reproduction Page 3

How to Use It: Give each student a copy of Reproduction Page 3. Each student then selects four numbers and places one in each corner position of the outside square in the array. Now fill in the blank circles on each side by subtracting the smaller number from the larger. These become the vertices of the next square. Repeat this process until the "Target" position is reached. The object of the game is to come as close to 0 as possible.

A display board can be provided in the classroom for students to post their results and see who can reach exactly 0. The following figure shows one example of a "Target" result of 0.

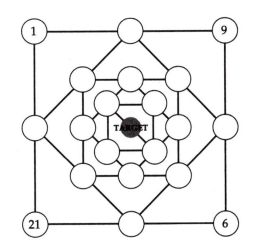

Teacher's Notes:

ACTIVITY 5   **Title:**   "Addition/Subtraction Slide Rule"

Purpose and Topic: This activity can be used to help students find sums and differences using a mechanical aid. Students should also develop an appreciation for some of the earlier attempts to create mechanical computing devices.

Materials: Reproduction Page 4

How to Make It: Have the students cut out the two scales shown on Reproduction Page 4.

How to Use It: Follow separate instructions for addition or subtraction.

Addition: Add 4 + 9 with the slide rule.

(a) Place the 0 on the A-scale directly above the 4 on the B-scale.
(b) Locate the 9 on the A-scale.
(c) Read the sum on the B-scale directly below the 9 on the A-scale: 4 + 9 = 13.

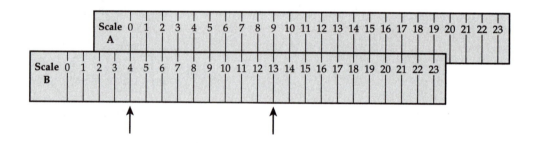

Subtraction: Subtract 19 – 6 with the slide rule.

(a) Place the 6 on the A-scale directly under the 19 on the B-scale.
(b) The answer is on the B-scale, directly above the 0 on the A-scale: 19 – 6 = 13.

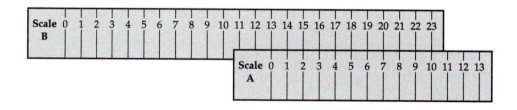

Extension: A palindrome is a word, sentence, or number that reads the same forward and backward. Thus, 22, 313, and 72027 are all palindromes. A palindrome can be formed from any number by using the "Reverse and

Add" technique—that is, by reversing the number and adding it to the original. This procedure may have to be repeated several times before a palindrome results; however, it provides excellent practice in addition. Here are several examples of this rule in action:

One Step	Two Steps	Four Steps
92	85	87
+ 29	+ 58	+ 78
121	143	165
	+ 341	+ 561
	484	726
		+ 627
		1353
		+ 3531
		4884

Now have your students try the "Reverse and Add" technique to find the palindromes for 184, 75, 156, 192, and 1069.

Problem: During a typical week at camp, the campers spend 21 hours swimming, 28 hours eating, 14 hours at computers, 7 hours at crafts, and 70 hours sleeping. The rest of the time is unscheduled, and the camp offers a selection of electives from which the children may choose.

(a) How many more hours are spent in swimming than in computers and crafts together?
(b) If these are the only scheduled activities, how many hours per week are left for electives?

Discussion:

(a) Campers spend 21 hours swimming, and $14 + 7 = 21$ hours in computers and crafts. Thus, they spend exactly the same amount of time in swimming as in computers and crafts together. Notice that, for this part of the problem, the 28 hours and the 70 hours are excess data.
(b) A week contains 7×24 or 168 hours. The scheduled activities take up $21 + 28 + 14 + 7 + 70 = 140$ hours. This leaves 28 hours for the elective activities.

Teacher's Notes:

ACTIVITY 6   **Title:**   "Roll 21"

Purpose and Topic: This activity provides students with practice in addition and subtraction of the integers; it also requires logical thought and decision making.

Materials: A pair of regulation dice

How to Use It: This game is played by two to five players. The object of the game is to achieve a total score of exactly 21. Each player begins with a score of 0. The students take turns rolling the pair of dice. Either die determines the operation (addition or subtraction); the other determines the number to be added to or subtracted from the player's total score. If an odd number occurs on one die, the student may choose to subtract the number that appears on the other. If an even number occurs on one die, the student may choose to add the number that appears on the other. For example, if the student rolls a 6 and a 3, he or she may subtract 6 from the total score (since the 3 is odd), or add 3 (since the 6 is even). If the numbers on both dice are even (odd), then the student has no option as to which operation to use. Thus, he or she must add (subtract) either number. For example, if the dice show 3 and 5, the student must subtract either the 3 or 5 from the total score. The object of the game is to score exactly 21. (*Note:* Students may go over 21, since they could obtain a subtraction situation on their next roll of the dice.)

Extension: An interesting variation for more advanced students is to include multiplication and division. Thus, an even number on a die permits either addition or multiplication; an odd number on a die permits subtraction or division. Notice that division will often lead to fractions, which must be compensated for by multiplication.

Problem 1:   Lauren made 20 bracelets out of blue and white beads. Some had 18 blue beads and 3 white beads. The rest had 12 blue beads and 9 white beads. How many beads did Lauren use altogether? How many beads of each color did she use to make the 20 bracelets?

Discussion: The first question, how many beads in all, can be answered by multiplying the number of bracelets (20) by the number of beads in each (21). Lauren used 420 beads. The second question cannot be answered with the given information. Have the students supply the missing information and find the answer.

Problem 2:   Twelve children each rode their bikes for 7 miles in a charity Bike-a-Thon. Five of them received pledges totaling $5 per mile. The remaining children had pledges that totaled $3 per mile. How much money did all 12 children raise for the charity altogether?

Discussion: The problem is solved by determining the amount of money earned by each of the two groups:

Group A: 5 children × $5 per mile × 7 miles = $175.00
Group B: 7 children × $3 per mile × 7 miles = $147.00
Total earned = $322.00

Teacher's Notes:

ACTIVITY 7   **Title:** "88"

Purpose and Topic: This game provides students with practice in mental addition and subtraction of integers.

Materials: A regular deck of 52 playing cards

How to Use It: This game is for three to five players. Begin by dealing three cards to each player. The rest of the deck is placed, face down, in the center of the table. Turn the top card in the deck face up in the center. Each player, in turn, places one of the cards from his hand, face up, on top of the upturned pile. The player then announces the sum of the cards in the pile at that point. Cards have the following values:

2 through 10 = face value
Ace = 1
Jack = 0
Queen = 10
King = –10

After a player puts down a card and announces the sum, he or she draws a replacement card from the face-down pack. All players should always have three cards in their hands. Play continues in this fashion. When a player is forced to announce a sum greater than 88, he or she is "out" and is eliminated from the game. Each player who goes over 88 is eliminated until only one player remains. This player is the winner.

Here is the beginning of a sample game with four players:

Card turned up to start:	7
Player #1 puts down a jack.	"The sum is 7."
Player #2 puts down a 6.	"The sum is 13."
Player #3 puts down a queen.	"The sum is 23."
Player #4 puts down a queen.	"The sum is 33."
Player #1 puts down a king.	"The sum is 23."
Player #2 puts down a 9.	"The sum is 32."
and so on.	

Play continues until, one by one, players exceed 88 and are eliminated.

Extension: Have the players explain their strategy of play. Which cards do they think are the most valuable? Why?

Problem 1: During what month does the middle day of the year occur?

Discussion: The middle day of a 365-day year is the 183rd day. Students should list the months, the number of days in each, and a running total of the number of days:

January	31	31
February	28	59
March	31	90
April	30	120
May	31	151
June	30	181
July	2	183

The middle or 183rd day will be during July.

Problem 2: Martha and Jackie each bought a pair of shoes. Together they spent $75. However, Martha spent $15 more than Jackie. How much did each girl spend for her pair of shoes?

Discussion: Guess and test reveals the answers to be $45 and $30. Algebraically, the equation $x + x + 15 = 75$ yields the same answers.

Problem 3: George sold 51 CDs in his first three days at the Record Shop. Each day he sold 3 more than he had sold the day before. How many CDs did he sell each day?

Discussion: Guess and test gives the answer of 14, 17, and 20. Logically, if George had sold the same number of CDs on each day, he would have sold 17 per day. Since he sold 3 more each day, it would be 14, 17, and 20.

Teacher's Notes:

ACTIVITY 8   **Title:**   "Napier Rods"

Purpose and Topic: These rods, sometimes called Napier Bones, are an illustration of an early computing device. Created by John Napier in 1617, they permit students to practice their basic multiplication facts in an addition model. Using these rods helps students see how the multiplication algorithm works and how place value enters into the multiplication process.

Materials: Reproduction Page 5 or a set of wooden tongue depressors

How to Make It: Reproduction Page 5 shows the set of Napier rods. These should be duplicated for each student and cut apart on the heavier lines, or they can be copied onto a set of tongue depressors.

How to Use It: Suppose you wish to multiply 432 × 4. Place the rods for 4, 3, and 2 next to each other. Align the Index rod at the left. The product is found along the diagonals by adding the numbers, as shown here:

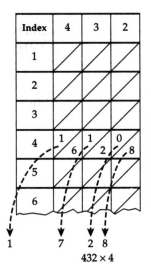

432 × 4

The use of these rods can be extended to multiplication by a two-digit multiplier. Suppose you want to multiply 432 × 53. Place the rods for 4, 3, and 2 next to each other with the Index rod at the left. Read the product of 432 × 3 (1296) and 432 × 5 (2160), as shown here:

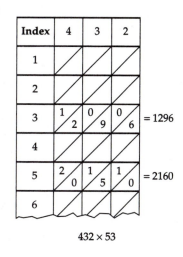

432 × 53

This second product is really 432 × 50, so you multiply 2160 by 10 (add a zero). You then add 21600 + 1296 = 22,896.

Problem 1: John spattered water on his multiplication homework and wiped out some of the digits. Complete John's problem by finding the missing digits.

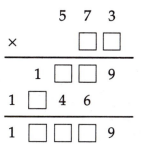

Discussion: Only 3 × 3 will yield 9, and only 3 × 2 will yield 6. Thus, the multiplier must be 23. Completing the problem will result as follows:

```
    573
  ×  23
   1719
   1146
  13179
```

Problem 2:   Michelle is a sponge diver at the local aquarium. She brings up 6 sponges on each dive. She made 2 dives on Friday, 5 dives on Saturday, and 3 dives on Sunday. How many sponges did she bring up on the 3 days?

Discussion: Students can use the distributive property of multiplication over addition:

$$6(2 + 5 + 3) = 6 \times 10 = 60$$

Or, they can find the number of sponges she brings up each day and add.

Problem 3:   There are 175 people waiting to take a boat ride from Vancouver to Victoria. Boat A holds 15 people, boat B holds 12 people, and boat C holds 8 people. Each boat makes the same number of trips. How many trips will each boat make?

Discussion: Each time the three boats make one trip, the total number of passengers is $15 + 12 + 8 = 35$. Since there are five 35s in 175, the boats must make 5 trips.

Teacher's Notes:

ACTIVITY 9   **Title:**   "Factor Game"

Purpose and Topic: This game provides practice in finding factors. It also gives students practice in using their multiplication and addition facts.

Materials: Reproduction Page 6

How to Use It: This game is played by two students. Each pair of students receives a copy of Reproduction Page 6, which contains the numbers from 1 through 50. Players decide who will go first (Player A) and who goes second (Player B). Player A selects a number from the array, writes it down as his score, and then crosses it off from the array. Player B now writes down all the factors of that number which are still in the array, and writes them down as her score. For example, if Player A chooses 49, Player B would get 7 and 1 for a total of 8 points, since 1 and 7 are the factors of 49. It is now Player B's turn to choose a number from the array and Player A receives any factors of that number that are still in the array for his score. Play continues in this fashion, with players adding their scores as they go. The game ends when all the numbers are gone from the array. The player with the higher total score is the winner. If time is a factor, the player with the higher score when time is called is the winner. Here is a sample beginning of a game:

	Player A	Player B
Player A selects 49 as his score:	49	
Player B receives 1 and 7 for her score:		8
Player B now selects 47 for her score:		47
Player A receives no factors (47 is prime):	—	
	49	55
Player A selects 27 as his score:	27	
Player B receives 3 and 9 as her score:		12
Player B now selects 15 as her score:		15
Player A receives 5 as his score (3 is gone):	5	
	81	82

Play continues in this fashion.

Extension: Adding a rule will make the game a bit more difficult. In order for a number to be picked, there must be at least one factor of that number left for the other player. Thus, if Player A selects 35, player B would get 1, 5, and 7. Now Player B could *not* select 49, since neither 7 nor 1 remains. Thus, 49 could never be selected. Player B could, however, select 14, since 2 is still on the board. This version of the game ends when neither player can make a move—that is, no numbers with factors remain on the board. The player with the higher score is the winner.

Problem 1:   Hot dog rolls usually come in packages of 12, whereas hot dogs usually come in packages of 8. At a barbecue you are giving, you need one roll for each hot dog. How many packages of hot dogs and how many packages of hot dog rolls must you buy to be certain there is an equal number of hot dogs and hot dog rolls?

Discussion: Students must find the common factors of 8 and 12 in order to find their least common multiple. Thus, the factors of 8 are 2, 2, and 2; the factors of 12 are 2, 2, and 3. One must buy $2 \times 2 \times 2 \times 3$, or 24 of each. Thus, one must buy 2 packages of rolls ($2 \times 12 = 24$) and 3 packages of hot dogs ($3 \times 8 = 24$). You might ask the students to determine the minimum number of packages of each they would buy if hot dogs came in packages of 7 and rolls in packages of 5.

Problem 2:   Four boys have ordered a pizza that has been cut into 8 equal parts. Just as they are about to eat, 2 more friends join them. What must they do in order for all 6 to have the same amount of the pizza?

Discussion: You need a number into which both 8 and 6 divide evenly. Thus, there must be 24 equal pieces. To do this, cut each of the 8 original slices into 3 equal parts, for a total of 24. Each boy now receives 1 1/3 of the original slices.
　　An alternate solution is to recognize that each person can begin by taking one of the original slices (6 in all). The remaining 2 slices are then divided up into 6 equal pieces (each slice is divided into 3).

Problem 3:   It takes Eli 12 minutes to walk one lap around the school track. It takes Judy 16 minutes to walk one lap. If they both begin to walk at 4:00 P.M., at what time will they finish a lap together?

Discussion: The least common multiple of 12 and 16 is 48. They will finish a lap together at 4:48 P.M.
　　Alternately, you can make two lists:

Eli	Judy
4:00	4:00
4:12	4:16
4:24	4:32
4:36	4:48
4:48	

Teacher's Notes:

ACTIVITY 10   **Title:** "Target"

Purpose and Topic: This activity provides students with practice in the fundamental operations of arithmetic with whole numbers. However, the order of operations and closure symbols (parentheses) must be used.

Materials: An ordinary deck of 52 playing cards

How to Make It: Remove the 12 face (picture) cards from the deck, leaving the cards marked 1 (ace) through 10. One deck is needed for each pair of students.

How to Use It: This game is played by pairs of students. The deck is shuffled and the top four cards are placed on the table, face up. The fifth card (the target card), is then turned face up. The first one who arranges the four cards with the proper symbols to yield the target card is the winner. There will probably be more than one correct answer to each problem. Here is an example:

Possible solutions include:

$(8 + 6 - 4) \div 2 = 5$
$(8 \div 4) + (6 \div 2) = 5$
$6 - [(8 \div 2) \div 4] = 5$

Extensions: You can extend the operations to include roots and powers. Another option is to change the number of cards being operated on from four to either three or five.

Problem 1:   Mark went into town to buy some photography equipment. He stopped at the bank and took $150 from his account. On his way home, he spent $100 for a camera, $25 for film, and $20 for a tripod. He returned home with $60. How much money did he have when he left home?

Discussion: Mark spent $145. He came home with $60. So, altogether he must have had $145 + $60, or $205. Since he took $150 from the bank, he must have started with $55.
Alternately, one can use some basic algebra:

Let n = the amount of money Mark started with
Then, $n + 150 - 100 - 25 - 20 = 60$
$$n + 150 - 145 = 60$$
$$n + 5 = 60$$
$$n = 55$$

Mark began with $55.

Problem 2:   The Charles family is driving from Philadelphia to Boston, a distance of 300 miles. They stopped for a picnic lunch exactly half way. Several hours later, Jerry Charles saw a sign that said "Boston—32 miles." How far had the family driven since lunch, when Jerry saw the sign?

Discussion: They had driven 118 miles:

$$300 - 150 = 150$$
$$150 - 32 = 118$$

Teacher's Notes:

ACTIVITY 11   **Title:**   "Wipeout"

Purpose and Topic: This activity helps students improve their computational abilities in a competitive game setting.

Materials: Chalkboard and chalk; two calculators; a deck of ordinary playing cards

How to Make It: Place the numbers from 1 through 50 on the chalkboard.

How to Use It: Divide the class into two teams. Teams alternate turns, with the next player on each team taking a turn. Provide one player on each team with a calculator. This can *only* be used to check the work of the other team. It may not be used during a particular team's turn.

   The deck of playing cards is shuffled and the teacher draws any three cards from the deck. The student whose turn it is may use one, two, or all three cards to make any number he or she wishes, providing it is still left in the array. (Numbers get "wiped out" as they are made.) Roots and powers may not be used. The team receives three points if the student uses all three cards, two points if she uses two cards, one point if she uses only one card, and zero points if she cannot make a number to be "wiped out." (*Note:* Either remove the picture cards or let pictures count as a 10.) For example, suppose the team pulls a 9, 10, and ace. They could make the following:

Three Points		**Two Points**		**One Point**
1	$(10 - 9) \times 1$	**11**	$(1 + 10)$	**1**
2	$(10 - 9 + 1)$	**19**	$(9 + 10)$	**9**
18	$(10 + 9 - 1)$			**10**
20	$(10 + 9 + 1)$			

and so on. The number formed can be checked by the player on the opposing team who has the calculator. If the work is correct, the team receives its points. If it is not correct, the team receives a 0 for that turn, and the game continues with the other team's turn. The game ends when all the numbers have been "wiped out" or when neither team can make a number for two successive turns.

Extension: Extend the game by using powers and square roots. In this situation, however, the exponent must be one of the three cards being used. For example, if the three cards are 7, 4, and 2:

$$(7 + 2)\sqrt{4} = 18$$
$$4^2 + 7 = 23$$
$$7^2 - 4 = 45$$

Problem 1:   Mrs. Drucker bought a set of tires for $252, a car vacuum cleaner for $24, and three gallons of antifreeze. Altogether she spent $300. How much did each gallon of antifreeze cost?

Discussion:

$$\$300 - \$252 = \$48$$
$$\$48 - \$24 = \$24$$
$$\$24 \div 3 = \$8$$

She paid $8 per gallon.

Problem 2:   Amanda's dad gave her a packet of stamps to start her stamp collection. A week later, her grandmother gave her 35 stamps. The following week she received 55 stamps from her aunt. After she had put all of these stamps into her new album, she found that she had 9 pages with 12 stamps on each page, and 3 pages with 8 stamps on each page. How many stamps did she get from her dad?

Discussion:

9 pages × 12 stamps	= 108 stamps
3 pages × 8 stamps	= 24 stamps
	132 stamps
grandmother	= 35 stamps
	97 stamps
aunt	= 55 stamps
	42 stamps

She received 42 stamps from her father.

Teacher's Notes:

ACTIVITY 12   **Title:**   "Score with 4"

Purpose and Topic: This game will help students master the four basic operations of arithmetic with whole numbers and closure symbols.

Materials: Reproduction Page 7

How to Use It: Divide the class into teams of three or four students. Give each team a copy of Reproduction Page 7. The team is to create a series of expressions, each of which has a value from 1 through 25. Each expression must contain the numbers 1, 2, 3, and 4 used only once, but in any order. Students may use addition, subtraction, multiplication, or division, as well as parentheses. The winning team is the first one to fill in all 25 blanks on the Reproduction Page with correct expressions. Although there are many answers for each number, here is one possible set:

$1 = (4 - 3) \times (2 - 1)$

$2 = (4 - 3) + (2 - 1)$

$3 = [(4 + 2) \div 3] + 1$

$4 = (4 - 2) + (3 - 1)$

$5 = (4 + 3) - (2 \times 1)$

$6 = (3 \times 4) \div (2 \times 1)$

$7 = (3 \times 4 \div 2) + 1$

$8 = 4 + 3 + 2 - 1$

$9 = (3 \times 4) - 2 - 1$

$10 = (3 \times 4) - (2 \times 1)$

$11 = (4 \times 3) - 2 + 1$

$12 = (4 \times 2) + 3 + 1$

$13 = 3 \times (4 + 1) - 2$

$14 = 4 \times (3 + 1) - 2$

$15 = (3 + 2) \times (4 - 1)$

$16 = 4 \times 2 \times (3 - 1)$

$17 = 3 \times (4 + 1) + 2$

$18 = (4 + 2) \times (3 \times 1)$

$19 = 4 \times (3 + 2) - 1$

$20 = (3 + 2) \times 4 \times 1$

$21 = (4 + 3) \times (2 + 1)$

$22 = 2 \times [(4 \times 3) - 1]$

$23 = (4 \times 3 \times 2) - 1$

$24 = 4 \times 3 \times 2 \times 1$

$25 = (4 \times 3 \times 2) + 1$

Extensions: Once the students have mastered the game with numbers from 1 through 25 using 1, 2, 3, and 4, you can extend the game to the numbers from 26 through 50, using 1, 2, 3, 4, and 5. Similarly, you can extend the game even further from 51 through 100 using the numbers 1, 2, 3, 4, 5, and 6.

Problem 1:   The school cafeteria received 146 bottles of juice in a delivery. Some of the bottles of juice came in 4-packs, the rest in 6-packs. How many of each type were delivered?

Discussion:

4 packs	35	32	29	26	. . .
6 packs	1	3	5	7	. . .

There are 12 possible combinations.

Problem 2:   In the school athletic program, there will be a tug-of-war held between two classes. Mrs. Ryan's class has 30 students, whereas Mr. Craig's class has 24 students. Each team in the tug-of-war must have the same number of students, and every student must be on exactly one team. What is the greatest number of students that can be on a team?

Discussion: The greatest common factor of 30 and 24 is 6. Mrs. Ryan's class will have five 6-person teams, while Mr. Craig's class will have four 6-person teams.

Problem 3:   At the golf club, there is a display case filled with golf balls. Any person who guesses the exact number wins a prize. Stan guessed 750, but he was off by 200. Luisa guessed 900, but she was off by 50. How many golf balls are in the display?

Discussion:

> If Stan was off by 200, there were either 550 or 950 golf balls.
> If Luisa was off by 50, there were either 950 or 850 golf balls.

Thus, there must have been 950 golf balls in the display.

Teacher's Notes:

ACTIVITY 13   **Title:** "Equation Search"

Purpose and Topic: Many magazines carry "word search" activities. These are letter grids with various word groupings hidden in them. This activity provides a review drill in the fundamental operations of arithmetic in a similar setting—one that is enjoyable to most students.

Materials: Reproduction Page 8

How to Make It: Provide each student with a copy of Reproduction Page 8 and a marker. At the same time, prepare an overhead transparency of the page. Of course, you can prepare a different array of numbers if desired.

How to Use It: Give each student a copy of Reproduction Page 8. Students are to discover as many as possible true mathematical equations within the grid by putting in the operational symbols and the equality symbol. Parentheses may also be used. Numbers can be used more than once, and equations can be made horizontally, vertically, or diagonally. Some of the possible answers for this grid are shown here:

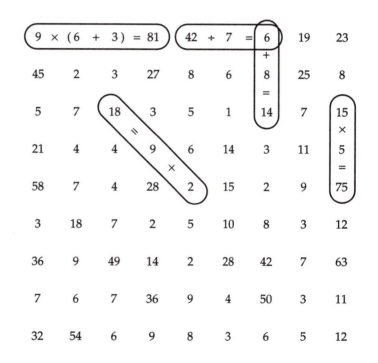

Students can place their own equations on the transparency for the entire class to see.

Problem 1:   Jonathan is practicing for the swimming team. Each week he adds 2 more laps to his schedule. During the fifth week he is swimming 12 laps. How many laps did he swim during the second week?

Discussion: Working backwards, you get 12 laps during the fifth week, 10 laps during the fourth week, 8 laps during the third week, and 6 laps during the second week.

Problem 2:   Arnold has five fish tanks, each with the same number of tropical fish. He gave one of the tanks to his sister, Barbara. Now he has 84 fish. How many fish did he start with?

Discussion: If Arnold has four tanks left and a total of 84 fish, each tank has 21 fish. He must have started with 5 × 21, or 105 tropical fish.

Teacher's Notes:

ACTIVITY 14   **Title:** "Put in the Signs"

Purpose and Topic: This activity provides students with practice in the use of the fundamental operations of arithmetic with whole numbers. It also provides review of the basic facts.

Materials: Reproduction Page 9

How to Use It: Have the students insert the proper operational signs to make both the rows (horizontal) and the columns (vertical) true statements. They must work from left to right and top to bottom. An answer key is given here:

7	−	2	+	5	=	10
−	■	+	■	−	■	−
10	÷	5	+	1	=	3
+	■	−	■	−	■	−
3	×	6	÷	3	=	6
=	■	=	■	=	■	=
0	+	1	+	1	=	1

6	÷	3	+	6	=	8
+	■	×	■	−	■	×
12	×	2	+	8	=	3
+	■	+	■	+	■	−
2	+	3	+	5	=	10
=	■	=	■	=	■	=
20	−	9	+	3	=	14

(*Note:* The lower right cell entry [i.e., 1 and 14] must satisfy both a row and a column.)

Extension: Have the students create their own "Put in the Signs" puzzles.

Problem 1:   Amanda has 72 baseball cards, and her brother, Ian, has 48. How many cards must Amanda give to Ian so that they each have the same number?

Discussion: Since Amanda has 24 more cards than Ian (72 − 48), she must give half of them (12) to Ian. They will each then have 60 cards.

Problem 2:   In the snack bar at the local mall, cashew nuts sell for $1.95 a bag and peanuts sell for 60¢ a bag. How many bags of peanuts can Sandy buy for the cost of one bag of cashew nuts?

Discussion: Divide 60¢ into $1.95. This gives 3 1/4. Thus, Sandy can buy three bags of peanuts.

Teacher's Notes:

ACTIVITY 15   **Title:** "Sieve of Eratosthenes"

Purpose and Topic: A topic that mathematicians have pursued through the ages is the development of a prime-producing expression. Eratosthenes was a Greek mathematician who lived about 230 B.C. His "sieve" is a mechanical method for locating all the prime numbers less than a given integer. The finished array will enable the students to identify primes as well as recognize the relationship between factors and multiples.

Materials: Reproduction Page 10

How to Use It: Give each student a copy of Reproduction Page 10. This lists all the numbers from 2 through 100. The students begin by putting a circle around the number 2, and then crossing out all the numbers that are multiples of 2. Now, have them circle the next number that is not crossed out (in this case, 3), and then cross out all the multiples of 3. Notice that some of these have already been crossed out since they were also multiples of 2. Have them continue by circling the next number not crossed out (5), and then crossing out all the multiples of 5. Have them continue in this manner, circling the next number not already crossed out, and then crossing out all of its multiples. When they have finished, they will have circled all of the primes between 2 and 100.

Ask the students why they think this configuration is called a "sieve." (A sieve is a strainer. This device "strains out" the prime numbers.)

Extensions: Ask the students to identify the pairs of "twin primes" they find. Twin primes are pairs of primes that differ by 2. There are exactly eight pairs of twin primes in the array given on Reproduction Page 10: 3 and 5, 5 and 7, 11 and 13, 17 and 19, 29 and 31, 41 and 43, 59 and 61, and 71 and 73. You might ask them to look for "prime triples" in this array (3, 5, and 7 are the only set—why?).

Encourage the students to look for patterns in their array. They should notice that many primes seem to be clustered about multiples of 6. Ask students if they can guess why this might happen.

Ask why there is only a single "even prime" (i.e., 2).

Are there more prime numbers between 2 and 100, or between 101 and 200? Have students prepare an array similar to their original sieve, but from 2 through 200. Have them go through the activity just as before, and then count the number of primes in each century.

Problem 1: Mrs. Janus bought some prizes for the students who were entered in the Science Fair. She spent $78 for them. Trophies cost $9 each and pins cost $4 each. If she bought the same number of pins as trophies, how many of each did she buy?

Discussion: Since she bought the same number of each, Mrs. Janus spent $13 for each pair. Thus, 78 ÷ 13 = 6 sets. She bought 6 pins ($24) and 6 trophies ($54).

Problem 2: There were 48 scouts at camp last week. They sleep in tents that can hold 3 scouts or tents that hold 4 scouts. All of the tents were full. How many tents were used? How many scouts were in each tent?

Discussion: There are five answers. Make a table:

3-scout tents	0	4	8	12	16
4-scout tents	12	9	6	3	0

Teacher's Notes:

ACTIVITY 16 **Title:** "Constructing Primes and Composites"

Purpose and Topic: Primes and composites have been the object of study for mathematicians for centuries. This activity enables students to construct a geometric model of prime and composite numbers.

Materials: 36 1" × 1" tiles, made of wood, plastic, poster-board, ceramic, etc.

How to Make It: Prepare an envelope/package with 36 tiles for each group of students. Provide each student with a copy of Reproduction Page 11.

How to Use It: Give each group of four students a package of the tiles. Each student should also have a copy of Reproduction Page 11. Have the students follow the instructions on the Reproduction Page to form rectangles and complete the table.

Number of Tiles	How Many Different Rectangles?	Dimensions	Area
2	1	1 × 2	2
3	1	1 × 3	3
4	2	1 × 4 2 × 2	4
5	1	1 × 5	5
6	2	1 × 6 2 × 3	6
7	1	1 × 7	7
8	2	1 × 8 2 × 4	8
9	2	1 × 9 3 × 3	9
10	2	1 × 10 2 × 5	10
11	1	1 × 11	11
12	3	1 × 12 2 × 6 3 × 4	12

The activity begins with two tiles, since 1 is neither a prime nor a composite. This should be discussed with your students.

Extensions: The lesson should be extended to include the concept of "factor pairs." Notice for any composite number, the dimensions of each rectangle represent a factor pair of that number. In the case of the square numbers, one of the factor pairs contains the same number twice, leading to the fact that the square numbers are the only numbers having an odd number of factors.
    Discuss the following with your students:

(a) When using 12 tiles, 3 rectangles resulted. What do these have in common? (They have the same area.)

(b) Do all rectangles with the same area have the same perimeter? (No. For example, using 4 tiles, the 2×2 rectangle has an area of 4 and a perimeter of 8, whereas the 1×4 rectangle has an area of 4 and a perimeter of 10.)

(c) Do all rectangles with the same perimeter have the same area? (No. For example, a 1×3 rectangle has a perimeter of 8 and an area of 3, whereas a 2×2 rectangle has a perimeter of 8 and an area of 4.)

Problem: A school has exactly 60 lockers and 60 students. On the first day of class, the students met in the school yard and came up with the following plan: The first student will enter the school and open all the lockers. The second student will then enter the school and close every locker with an even number $(2, 4, 6, \dots)$. The third student will then enter and "reverse" every third locker $(3, 6, 9, \dots)$. That is, if the locker is closed he or she will open it; if it is open, he or she will close it. The fourth student will then reverse every fourth locker $(4, 8, 12, \dots)$, and so on until all 60 students have reversed the proper lockers. Which lockers will finally remain open?

Discussion: This problem could be resolved by getting 60 students and 60 lockers, and actually "doing" the problem. However, one can reduce the complexity of the problem and see if a pattern emerges. Assume, for example, that there were 20 lockers. Then take 20 students, provide them with large cards numbered from 1 to 20, and let them represent the lockers. Facing forward will be considered "open" and facing away will be considered to be "closed." The students then act out the story in the problem.

You may also construct a table, in which O represents an open locker and C represents a closed locker. The table will readily reveal that the lockers numbered 1, 4, 9, and 16 will remain open, whereas all others will be closed.

Locker #	1	2	3	4	5	6	7	8	9	10	11	12	13	14	15	16	17	18	19	20
Student 1	O	O	O	O	O	O	O	O	O	O	O	O	O	O	O	O	O	O	O	O
2		C	O	C	O	C	O	C	O	C	O	C	O	C	O	C	O	C	O	C
3			C	C	O	O	O	C	C	C	O	O	O	C	C	C	O	O	O	C
4				O	O	O	O	O	C	C	O	C	O	C	C	O	O	O	O	O
5					C	O	O	O	C	O	O	C	O	C	O	O	O	O	O	C
6						C	O	O	C	O	O	O	O	C	O	O	O	C	O	C
7							C	O	C	O	O	O	O	O	O	O	O	C	O	C
8								C	C	O	O	O	O	O	O	C	O	C	O	C
9									O	O	O	O	O	O	O	C	O	O	O	C
10										C	O	O	O	O	O	C	O	O	O	O
11											C	O	O	O	O	C	O	O	O	O
12												C	O	O	O	C	O	O	O	O
13													C	O	O	C	O	O	O	O
14														C	O	C	O	O	O	O
15															C	C	O	O	O	O
16																O	O	O	O	O
17																	C	O	O	O
18																		C	O	O
19																			C	O
20																				C

Once the problem has been resolved, you should discuss with your students why this happens. This relates directly to the activity they have previously done, in that it is a lesson dealing with factors. For example, consider locker number 12: The students who will touch this locker occur in pairs: 1 and 12, 2 and 6, and 3 and 4 (a total of 6 factors or students). However, if you consider locker number 16, you obtain 1 and 16, 2 and 8, and 4 (a total of 5 factors or students). As the students saw in their earlier work, only the perfect squares have an odd number of factors, resulting in the open status of the lockers with those numbers.

Teacher's Notes:

ACTIVITY 17   **Title:**   "I Have...Who Has...?

Purpose and Topic: In this activity, students are given an opportunity to review many of their arithmetic and algebraic operations and concepts in a game setting. In addition, the activity encourages mental arithmetic as well as listening skills.

Materials: A deck of 3" × 5" cards, or a similar deck made from poster-board

How to Make It: Prepare a deck of cards, providing at least one card for each child in your class. On each card, write a number followed by a mathematical question. The answer to this question will be the number on another card. The final card will have the question that cycles back to the first card. (See the sample decks below).

How to Use It: Begin the game by shuffling the deck to make certain that the cards are not in order. Distribute the cards at random, one at a time, to the students. Keep one card for yourself. Each student should have at least one card. If there are more cards than students, some will receive two cards. Instruct the students to pay strict attention, since they must respond when their number is the answer to the given question or when someone makes an error. Computations can be done with pencil and paper (if necessary), but mental arithmetic is preferable. Students must listen carefully. You (the teacher) begin the game by reading the question on your card. Then the cycle begin as students respond.

Here are three sample decks. Deck #1 contains 25 cards; Deck #2 contains 27 cards; and Deck #3 contains 27 cards. This number is arbitrary; adjust the number of cards to fit your own class size. Be careful that no two cards lead to the same answer.

Deck #1

I have 40. Who has my number plus 8?

I have 48. Who has my number divided by 4?

I have 12. Who has my number divided by 3 then increased by 6?

I have 10. Who has 5 times my number?

I have 50. Who has 5 less than my number?

I have 45. Who has 12 less than one-third of my number?

I have 3. Who has twice as much?

I have 6. Who has 2 more than twice my number?

I have 14. Who has 1 more than half my number?

I have 8. Who has 3 times as much?

I have 24. Who has my number divided by 6?

I have 4. Who has 3 more than 3 times my number?

I have 15. Who has twice my number?

I have 30. Who has 1 less than my number divided by 5?

I have 5. Who has 3 more than 3 times my number?

I have 18. Who has one-half as much?

I have 9. Who has 1 less than 4 times my number?

I have 35. Who has my number divided by 5?

I have 7. Who has 6 more than twice my number?

I have 20. Who has twice my number increased by 1?

I have 41. Who has my number increased by 1/2 of 2?

I have 42. Who has my number divided by 2?

I have 21. Who has my number diminished by 5?

I have 16. Who has twice as much?

I have 32. Who has my number increased by 8?

Deck #2

I have 7. Who has 4 more than 3 times my number?

I have 25. Who has 2 less than the square root of my number?

I have 3. Who has twice the square of my number?

I have 18. Who has 10 less than one-half of my number?

I have –1. Who has my number cubed then subtract 4?

I have –5. Who has negative 3 times my number then add 1?

I have 16. Who has 10 less than the square root of my number?

I have –6. Who has 3 more than twice my number?

I have –9. Who has 1 less than the absolute value of my number?

I have 8. Who has the square root of 2 times my number?

I have 4. Who has 4 less than one-half this number?

I have –2. Who has 5 less than 5 times my number?

I have –15. Who has 7 more than my number divided by 3?

I have 2. Who has 2 less than my number cubed?

I have 6. Who has 2 more than one-half my number?

I have 5. Who has the cube of my number?

I have 125. Who has one-half more than one-half of my number?

I have 63. Who has one-third of my number?

I have 21. Who has its double?

I have 42. Who has my number diminished by the square root of 25?

I have 37. Who has my number decreased by the square root of 169?

I have 24. Who has my number decreased by 3^3?

I have –3. Who has my number squared?

I have 9. Who has my number squared?

I have 81. Who has my number increased by 19?

I have 100. Who has the square root of my number?

I have 10. Who has my number minus 3?

Deck #3

I have 16. Who has 4 1/2 times my number?

I have 72. Who has the square of the sum of my digits?

I have 81. Who has 27 less than my number?

I have 54. Who has my number diminished by the product of 2 and 11?

I have 32. Who has 1/3 the product of my digits?

I have 2. Who has 3 more than my cube?

I have 11. Who has 7 more than twice my number?

I have 29. Who has the product of my digits?

I have 18. Who has 100 minus 4 times my number?

I have 28. Who has the sum of the squares of my digits?

I have 68. Who has 19 less than my number?

I have 49. Who has a dozen more than my square root?

I have 19. Who has the next prime number?

I have 23. Who has the difference between my number and 50?

I have 27. Who has the cube root of my number?

I have 3. Who has the next larger number of which my number is a factor?

I have 6. Who has 4 less than the cube of my number?

I have 212. Who has the sum of the squares of my digits?

I have 9. Who has 4 more than the product of my number and 12?

I have 112. Who has one-half my number?

I have 56. Who has the sum of all my factors?

I have 120. Who has the difference between my number and 11^2?

I have 1. Who has 14 more than my number raised to the 5th power?

I have 15. Who has my number diminished by an even prime number?

I have 13. Who has my number increased by the square root of 8^2?

I have 21. Who has my number increased by the product of 5 and 2^3?

I have 61. Who has my number with the digits reversed?

Extensions: Try these variations:

 (a) Deck #2 and Deck #3 could easily be used with algebra classes, or a deck could be constructed for a geometry class.

 (b) Divide the class into groups of four students. Have each group create a deck. The mathematical content of the deck will be determined by the mathematics being learned. This raises the level of the entire activity, since students must now create questions as well as their answers. They must then put them into a sequence, keeping in mind that all the answers must be different; otherwise, two questions could lead to the same answer.

Problem: When the class used Mary's deck of 24 cards, they found that several students responded many times, yet other students did not respond at all. Why?

Discussion: If two questions yield the same answer, two "loops" result: responders and nonresponders. Explore this situation by creating a deck in which two questions have the same answer. Play the game several times, shuffling the deck each time. Keep a record of the number of students in each "loop."

Teacher's Notes:

ACTIVITY 18   **Title:**   "COMPU"

Purpose and Topic: This activity is designed to improve students' computational skills with whole numbers in a game setting.

Materials: Reproduction Page 12; Reproduction Page 13; 10 number cards

How to Make It: Place the numbers from 1 through 10, each on a separate 3" × 5" card, or take one set of cards, ace through 10, from an ordinary deck of playing cards. Make sufficient copies of Reproduction Page 12 for each student to have one.

How to Use It: Follow these steps:

  (a) Give each student a COMPU board from Reproduction Page 12. Have them fill in the 24 blank squares on the card with their choice of numbers as follows: under the C, from 1 through 18; under the O, from 19 through 36; under the M, from 37 through 55; under the P, from 56 through 72; and under the U, from 73 through 90. (*Note:* The "FREE" space need not be filled in.)
  (b) Place the 10 number cards in a box. Shake well. Select any two cards at random and reveal the numbers to the class. Students may add, subtract, multiply, or divide to get an answer. If the result appears on their card, they circle the answer and then write the operation used in that same box. (*Note:* In subtraction, only absolute value is used. In division, only whole number results are accepted.) Thus, for each pair of numbers shown, a student could possibly have as many as three or four numbers on his or her number card circled.
  (c) The teacher, or a student chosen by the teacher, keeps track of the number pairs drawn on the Master List, Reproduction Page 13. Enter each number pair as it is drawn, and fill in the remaining four columns. This serves as a check to determine the accuracy of the student winners.
  (d) Place the two number cards back in the box, mix well, and pick the next two cards. Continue in this manner until some student gets COMPU, which is five boxes in a row, horizontally, vertically, or diagonally.

  Here is an example: You select a 5 and a 2. Students examine their cards and they can circle 7 (5 + 2), 3 (5 − 2), or 10 (5 × 2), if any of those numbers are on their cards. There is no division permitted since 5 ÷ 2 does not yield a whole number. Or perhaps you select a 4 and an 8. Students may circle 12 (4 + 8), 4 (8 − 4), 32 (8 × 4), or 2 (8 ÷ 4).

Extension: For children with more experience, use cards with the numbers from 11 through 20. The game is played in exactly the same manner.

Problem 1:   During the spring vacation, two families went to a baseball game. There were more children than adults. Tickets cost $12 for adults and $9 for children. The two families spent $90 on admission. How many people were in the group?

Discussion: Have your students make a table and use guess and test. There were 3 adults and 6 children.

Problem 2:   There are 29 students who take part in athletics. Of these, 16 are on the softball team, 11 are on the basketball team, and 4 of these are on both. The rest of the students are on the volleyball team. How many students are on the volleyball team?

Discussion: There are 16 students on the softball team and 11 on the basketball team; 4 of these are on both. Therefore, there are 12 students who are *only* on the softball team, 7 who are *only* on the basketball team, and 4 who are on both, for a total of 23. This leaves 6 students on the volleyball team.

Teacher's Notes:

ACTIVITY 19   **Title:** "Multiplo"

Purpose and Topic: This activity provides students with practice in using multiples and factors in a game setting.

Materials: A deck of 36 square cards; Reproduction Pages 14 and 15; a game board (optional)

How to Make It: Prepare a deck of 36 cards. You may cut out the cards shown on Reproduction Pages 14 and 15, or prepare a deck of your own. Each card is to have a composite number on the top and right side, and a single digit on the bottom and left side. Four sample cards are shown on page 43.

In addition, a game board can be constructed by ruling 36 squares (i.e., it should contain the 36 cards in a 6 × 6 array). Each square on the game board should be slightly larger than the cards being used.

How to Use It: The game can be played by two to four players. Each player is dealt six cards. The unused cards are placed face down in the center. The first player places any card from his or her hand near the center of the board. Each subsequent player, in turn, must place one of his or her cards onto the board, adjacent to a card or cards already placed on the table. The card placed must have its adjacent edges either multiples or factors of the numbers they touch on the adjacent card or cards.

If a player cannot find such a card in his or her hand, he or she must pick from the deck until a play can be made. If the deck is exhausted, the player passes the turn to the next player. The game ends when one player has played all the cards in his or her hand, or if no further play is possible. The winner is the person with the highest score.

Scoring is as follows:

If a play matches one edge, the player receives 1 point.

If a play matches two edges, the player receives 3 points.

If a play matches three edges, the player receives 6 points.

If a play matches four edges, the player receives 10 points.

If a player uses up all the cards in his hand, a 25 point bonus is scored.

When play ends, players must deduct 1 point for every card remaining in their hand.

Here is a sample round of 4 cards.

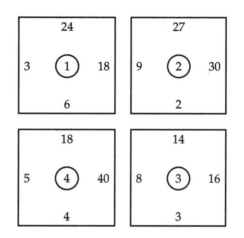

Player #1 scores 0 (no matches possible, since this is the first card played).

Player #2 scores 1 point, since the 18 and the 9 are a match.

Player #3 scores 1 point, since the 2 and the 14 are a match.

Player #4 scores 3 points since the 8 and 40 are a match, and the 6 and 18 are also a match.

Problem 1:   There were 300 students and teachers signed up for the trip to Washington, DC. Each bus holds 33 people. The principal ordered 9 buses. When all of the buses were filled, there were still some students left over. What's wrong?

Discussion: Divide 33 into 300. The result is 9.090909.... The principal rounded this down to 9. This is arithmetically correct, but practically wrong.

Problem 2:   It was Kid's Day at the ballpark. Every child aged 12 and under received a miniature bat. The first 50 children were also given a ticket, with a number from 1 through 50. At the drawing held during the seventh-inning stretch, prizes were awarded as follows: Every child whose ticket had a number that was a multiple of 4 received a T-shirt. Every child whose ticket had a number that was a multiple of 6 received a team cap. How many children received exactly one prize? How many received exactly two prizes? How many received exactly three prizes?

Discussion: There were 4 children who received three prizes; 12 who received two prizes; and 34 who received one prize.

Each of the children received a bat. Make a list of the multiples of 6 and the multiples of 4. Notice that numbers 12, 24, 36, and 48 are on both lists. These are the people who received all three prizes.

Teacher's Notes:

CHAPTER TWO

Fractions, Decimals, and Percents

ACTIVITY 20　**Title:**　"Fraction Wheel"

Purpose and Topic:　This device provides a hands-on means for visualizing a fraction as a part of a circular region.

Materials:　Reproduction Page 16; a pair of scissors

How to Make It:　Give each pair of students a copy of Reproduction Page 16 and a pair of scissors. Have them cut out the two circles. Then cut along the radius in each circle as shown. Insert circle B into circle A along the cuts.

How to Use It:　One student in each pair should draw a circle and shade in what he or she thinks 1/3 of the circle would be. Now open the Fraction Wheel to 1/3, as shown on page 46. How does the estimate compare with the actual fraction? Do the same for other fractions less than 1.

Extension:　This same model can be used to illustrate angle measure by replacing the fractions on the circle by degrees from 0° through 360°. For example, 1/3 will be replaced by 120°; 1/4 by 90°; and so on.

Problem:　In the Carson Middle School, 1/2 of the sixth-grade students went to the Sports Club meeting, 1/3 of the sixth-grade students went to the Art Club meeting, and 1/6 of the sixth-grade students went to the Music Club meeting. Make a circle graph to show this data.

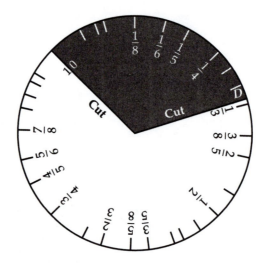

Discussion: Use the Fraction Wheel to determine each of the three regions. Note that each new region begins where the previous region ended.

Teacher's Notes:

ACTIVITY 21   **Title:**   "Fraction Go Fish"

Purpose and Topic: Most students enjoy the competitive nature of card games. This activity is an adaptation of a traditional card game that provides the opportunity for students to review equivalent fractions.

Materials: A pack of twenty-six 3" × 5" cards

How to Make It: On each card, write one of the following common fractions:

1/2	1/4	1/3	1/5	2/8	2/10	4/12	3/9
	2/4	2/3	2/5	4/8	4/10	6/12	5/15
	3/4	2/6	3/5	6/8	6/10	9/12	12/16
		3/6	4/5		8/10		
		4/6					

How to Use It: This game can be played by two or three players. One student is designated as dealer. He or she shuffles the deck and then deals five cards to each player. The rest of the deck is placed face down on the table as a "pack." All players begin by discarding any equivalent pairs they may have in their hands. These are placed face up, alongside the pack. The first player (the dealer) asks any other specific player if he or she has a particular card that enables the first player to make a pair. For example, player #1 might have a card with 12/16 on it. He or she then might ask player #3, "Do you have a card with 3/4 on it?" If player #3 has a card with 3/4, *or any equivalent*, he or she must give it to player #1, who then discards the equivalent pair. Player #1 then continues asking for another card.

If a player does not have the requested card, the player asking must "Go Fish." That is, the player draws the top card from the pack and places it in his or her hand. Play then passes to the next player.

If the pack is depleted, play continues with players simply asking each other for cards needed to make equivalent pairs.

The game ends when one player discards all the cards in his or her hand by throwing out pairs of equivalent fractions. If no one succeeds in discarding all cards, the winner is the player with the fewest cards remaining when time is called.

Extensions: Several variations of this game can be made:

(a) A player who is "fishing" from the pack must continue picking cards until he or she can make any equivalent pair. That pair is discarded and play continues as before.

(b) This variation is played as in the original with the only change being that equivalent pairs are placed in front of the respective players. At the end of the game, the player with the most pairs is the winner.

Problem 1:   Two fractions each equal 2/3 when reduced to lowest terms. The difference between the numerator and denominator of one fraction is 5. The difference between the numerator and the denominator of the other fraction is 7. What are the two fractions?

Discussion: List the set of fractions equivalent to 2/3:

2/3, 4/6, 6/9, 8/12, **10/15,** 12/18, **14/21**

Problem 2:   There are 240 animals on a farm. One-half of them are horses, one-third are pigs, and the rest are chickens. How many of the animals are chickens?

Discussion:
1/2 × 240 = 120 (horses)
1/3 × 240 = 80 (pigs)
120 + 80 = 200, leaving 40 for the number of chickens

A more sophisticated approach would be as follows:

1/2 + 1/3 = 5/6

Therefore, the remaining 1/6 are the chickens.

1/6 × 240 = 40, the number of chickens

Teacher's Notes:

ACTIVITY 22   **Title:**   "Beat the Fraction"

Purpose and Topic: This game involves comparing fractions. The mathematics of this game is ordering fractions.

Materials: A deck of thirty-six 3" × 5" cards for each group of players

How to Make It: On each card, write one of the following fractions:

1/2	1/3	2/3	1/4	2/4	3/4	1/5	2/5	3/5	4/5
1/6	2/6	3/6	4/6	5/6	1/8	2/8	3/8	4/8	5/8
6/8	7/8	1/9	3/9	6/9	8/9	9/9	1/10	2/10	3/10
4/10	5/10	6/10	7/10	8/10	9/10				

How to Use It: The game can be played by two, three, or four players. Shuffle the deck and deal four cards, one at a time, to each player. The remaining cards are placed in a pack, face down in the center. The first player places any one of his or her cards on the table, face up. Succeeding players, in turn, must select one card from their hand and place it face up on the table. The player with the card showing the fraction of greatest value takes all the played cards from that round. These are placed in front of that player as a "bank." Each player now picks one card from the pack to replace the card that was played. Play continues with each player in turn, leading off a round. When no more cards remain in the pack, each person plays cards from his or her hand without replacement. Play ends when all the cards in the players' hands have been exhausted. The winner is the player with the most cards in his or her bank.

Extension: The game can be extended to a "Make a Whole Number." In this version, players take turns selecting a card from their hands and playing it on the table. The objective is to use the cards on the table to form a sum that is a whole number. For example, player #1 puts down 1/4. Player #2 puts down 1/4. Player #3 has a 1/2 card, which he or she plays on top and announces "1/4 + 1/4 + 1/2 = 1." This player removes the three cards and places them in his or her bank. Each time a player places a card on the table, it is replenished with a pick from the pack. Players continue taking turns, until all the cards have been exhausted.

Problem 1:   The rainfall during three summer months in a small, desert town was 1 1/4", 1/2", and 3/4". If the annual rainfall in this town averages 6 1/4", how much more rain can be expected?

Discussion: This is an example of a two-stage problem. Students must first add the rainfall from the three months (2 1/2") and then subtract this sum from the 6 1/4". The result, 3 3/4", is the required amount.

Problem 2:   Joanne went on a camera-safari last January; 3/4 of her pictures were of animals. Of these, 1/2 were of elephants. What part of her pictures were not elephants?

Discussion: Again, this is a multistage problem. Taking 1/2 of 3/4 reveals that 3/8 of Joanne's pictures were of elephants. This means 5/8 of her pictures were *not* elephants.

Teacher's Notes:

ACTIVITY 23   **Title:**   "FRIO: Fractions in Order"

Purpose and Topic: This game will help students determine the order of magnitude of various fractions. It will also provide practice in determining the lowest common denominator for two or more fractions.

Materials: A deck of twenty-six 3" × 5" cards; a list of fractions in correct order

How to Make It: On each of the 3" × 5" cards, write one of the following fractions:

1/10	2/10	3/10	4/10	5/10	6/10	7/10	8/10	9/10
1/8	2/8	3/8	4/8	5/8	6/8	7/8	1/3	2/3
1/5	2/5	3/5	4/5	1/4	2/4	3/4	1/2	

Prepare a list of these fractions in order of magnitude. This list is for a student who will act as judge if any question arises.

1/10, 1/8, 1/5 or 2/10, 1/4 or 2/8, 3/10, 1/3, 3/8, 2/5 or 4/10, 1/2 or 2/4 or 4/8 or 5/10, 3/5 or 6/10, 5/8, 2/3, 7/10, 6/8 or 3/4, 4/5 or 8/10, 7/8, 9/10

How to Use It: The game with 26 cards is best suited for two players but can be extended to three players. The deck is shuffled and each player is dealt one card at a time, *face up in a row,* on the table, until each player has received 5 cards. The rest of the deck (called the "pack"), is placed *face down* in the middle of the table, between the players. Each player must keep the cards he or she was dealt in front of him or her *in the order in which they were dealt; cards may not be interchanged.*

The object of the game is for the 5 cards in front of the player to be in ascending order. Each player, in turn, may either draw a card from the pack or take the top card from the discard pile. If the new card will help to get the 5 cards in order, the player keeps it and exchanges it for one of his or her own cards. The new card is placed face up in the same position as the card it replaces. The replaced card is discarded, face up, in the center, on top of the discard pile. For example, suppose a player is dealt the following:

On his first turn, the player draws 2/8. He replaces the 2/3 with it. On his next turn, he sees a 1/8 on top of the discard pile but chooses to draw instead. He draws a 2/4 card and replaces the 7/8. His hand now looks like this:

Now all the player needs is a card to replace the 1/10 between the 2/4 and the 3/4. When he does that, his 5 cards are in order, and so he calls "FRIO" and wins the game.

Extension: The game can be extended so that the objective is to have the 5 cards in front of a player either be in ascending or descending order.

Problem 1:   The same nonzero, positive number is added to the numerator and denominator of a fraction. Will the new fraction be greater than, equal to, or less than the original fraction?

Discussion: If the original fraction has a value less than 1, the new fraction will be greater than the original:

$$3/5 > 4/6 > 5/7 \ldots$$

If, however, the original fraction has a value greater than 1, then the new fraction will have a value less than the original:

$$5/3 < 6/4 < 7/5 \ldots$$

Problem 2:   The Little League baseball season was just concluded. Each team played the same number of games. The Bearcats won 3/4 of their games. The Cougars won 2/3 of their games. The Demons won 4/6 of their games. Who won the most games?

Discussion: Students should order the three fractions by finding the common denominator, 12.

$$3/4 = 9/12 \qquad 2/3 = 8/12 \qquad 4/6 = 8/12$$

The Bearcats won the most games.

Problem 3:   If each team in the previous problem played a total of 36 games, how many games did each team win?

Discussion :
   3/4 of 36 = 27 (won by the Bearcats)
   2/3 of 36 = 24 (won by the Cougars)
   4/6 of 36 = 24 (won by the Demons)

Teacher's Notes:

ACTIVITY 24   **Title:** "Tangram Fractions"

Purpose and Topic: Tangrams are an extremely versatile device. They offer an opportunity for students to solve problems, engage in creative activities, and use their imaginations. Although tangrams are usually thought of in connection with geometry activities (you will find additional activities with tangrams in Activity 41), this activity focuses on using the tangrams to compare fractional parts as well as adding and subtracting fractions.

Materials: Reproduction Page 17; a pair of scissors

How to Make It: Give each student a copy of Reproduction Page 17 or make copies of the page on light cardboard, oak-tag, or poster-board. Have the students cut out the seven pieces of the tangram set.

How to Use It: Follow these steps:

(a) Assign the value 1 to the original square. Challenge the students to find the value of each of the seven pieces, as shown here:

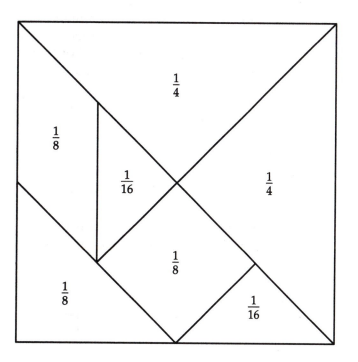

(b) Have the students make figures of their own, using some or all of the pieces in their set. Outline their figures on a separate sheet of paper. Have other students attempt to find the value for each of these figures. Have them determine how much more one figure is than another.

(c) See how many different shapes the students can make having a given value such as 3/8, 5/8, 7/8, and so on.

Extension: Ask the students to work in small groups and attempt to make a square using exactly 1 piece, 2 pieces, 3 pieces, and so on, all the way up to 7 pieces (the original square). Can they make all of them? Have students explain their solutions to the entire class using an overhead projector. Find the value of each square.

Problem 1:   A veterinarian begins work each day at 8:00 A.M. She has fifteen 1/2-hour appointments, and takes 3/4 of an hour for her lunch. When does her day end?

Discussion: Fifteen 1/2-hour appointments take 7 1/2 hours. Add the 3/4 of an hour she takes for her lunch, and her total day is 8 1/4 hours, or 8 hours and 15 minutes. Add this to 8:00 A.M. She finishes her day at 4:15 P.M.

Problem 2:   Ken spent one-half of his savings to buy a baseball glove. He then spent $12.50 for a bat and the remaining $25.00 for spikes. How much did he pay for the baseball glove?

Discussion: Since Ken spent one-half of his money for the glove, the rest of his purchases must be the other one-half. Thus, he spent $12.50 + $25.00, or $37.50 for the glove.

Teacher's Notes:

ACTIVITY 25   **Title:**   "Fraction Magic Squares"

Purpose and Topic: This activity provides practice in adding and subtracting fractions.

Materials: Reproduction Page 18

How to Use It: Distribute a copy of Reproduction Page 18 to each student. Discuss with the class the meaning of a "Magic Square." Show how the sum of the three addends must be the same horizontally, diagonally, and vertically. The sum of each row, diagonal, and column is referred to as the "magic sum." In each case, students are to complete the magic square and give the magic sum. You might wish to do the first one with the class, as an example.

	$2\frac{1}{6}$	
$2\frac{1}{3}$	$2\frac{7}{18}$	$2\frac{1}{9}$

By adding the terms in the bottom row, the magic sum is 6 5/6. You now proceed by finding the missing center cell, followed by the upper right cell. The finished magic square is as follows:

$2\frac{4}{9}$	$2\frac{1}{6}$	$2\frac{2}{9}$
$2\frac{1}{18}$	$2\frac{5}{18}$	$2\frac{1}{2}$
$2\frac{1}{3}$	$2\frac{7}{18}$	$2\frac{1}{9}$

The completed magic squares as shown on the Reproduction Page are as follows:

1	3½	3
4½	2½	½
2	1½	4

Magic sum = <u>7½</u>

1⅓	1	2⅔
3	1⅔	⅓
⅔	2⅓	2

Magic sum = <u>5</u>

⅖	2⁹⁄₁₀	1⅕
2³⁄₁₀	1½	⁷⁄₁₀
1⅘	¹⁄₁₀	2⅗

Magic sum = <u>4½</u>

Extension: Have the students create their own magic squares. It is probably best if you begin by using only whole numbers and then extend to fractions.

Problem 1: In a science experiment, the teacher dropped a golf ball from the top of a 48-foot tower onto the concrete floor. Each time the ball hits the floor, it rebounds to a height that is 3/4 of the previous height. What height will it reach after the fourth bounce?

Discussion: Students may wish to make a drawing or a table as follows:

Bounce #	Rebound Height
1	36 feet
2	27 feet
3	20 1/4 feet
4	15 3/16 feet

Other students may recognize that the answer can be expressed as:

(3/4)(3/4)(3/4)(3/4)(48)
243/16 = 15 3/16

Problem 2:   At the school fair, the big attraction is the jump rope contest between the two sixth-grade classes. Miss Schiavone's class has 35 students and Mr. Lepow's class has 28 students. Every team in the contest must have the same number of students, and every student must be on exactly one team. What is the greatest number of students that can be on each team? How many teams will there be?

Discussion: The greatest common factor of 28 and 35 is 7. There will be 7 students on each jump rope team. Miss Schiavone's class will have 5 teams; Mr. Lepow's class will have 4 teams.

Teacher's Notes:

ACTIVITY 26   **Title:** "Make a Proportion"

Purpose and Topic: This game utilizes the fact that in a proportion, the product of the means equals the product of the extremes. In addition, it provides practice for the student in determining equivalent fractions.

Materials: A deck of thirty-six 3" × 5" cards (or a deck of playing cards with the 10s and face cards removed); Reproduction Page 19

How to Make It: Place the numbers 1 through 9 on individual cards. Make four sets.

How to Use It: This game is played by two players. Reproduction Page 19 shows a playing mat. This is placed on the table between the two players. Shuffle the deck and deal 8 cards to each player. The remaining 20 cards are placed face down on the mat.

  The first player takes any 2 cards from his hand and places them face up in any two positions on the mat. The player now replaces the two cards in his hand by drawing the top 2 cards from the pack. The second player must now use two cards from her hand to form equivalent fractions (i.e., a proportion). These cards are also replaced by drawing from the pack. If the second player makes a proportion, she takes the 4 cards from the mat and places them in her bank. She now places the first 2 cards onto the mat for the next proportion. If she cannot make a proportion, the first player has an opportunity to do so. If neither player can form a proportion, the 2 cards on the mat are placed at the bottom of the pack to be used again. Play continues with the second player now placing the first 2 cards from her hand. At all times, players should have 8 cards in their hands until the pack is depleted. When the pack is gone, play continues without replacement. The game ends when a proportion cannot be made by either player or when one player has no cards left. The winner is the player with the most cards in his or her bank. (*Note:* The person attempting to make the proportion can use double digits in either or both positions—for instance, use 8 and 4 to make 48 or 84.) Here are a couple of examples:

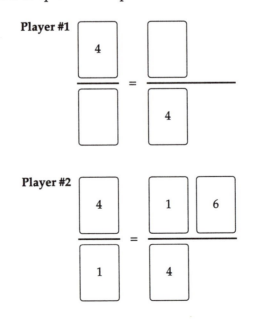

Extensions:
 (a) In this extension, players alternate turns placing one card at a time on the mat. If the second player on his or her second turn (the fourth card) cannot form a proportion, then the players alternate turns picking one card at a time from the pack until one of them forms a proportion.
 (b) A modification of the game is to allow the players, when their turn comes, to change the position of the cards already on the table.

Problem 1:   A recipe for salsa says to use 2 teaspoons of hot peppers for 16 ounces of salsa. Maury is making 36 ounces of salsa for a party. How much hot peppers will he need?

Discussion: Students should form a proportion as follows:

$$\frac{2}{16} = \frac{x}{36}$$

from which students will find that Maury needs 4 1/2 teaspoons of hot peppers.

Problem 2:   Suzanne is cutting out stars to make flags. Each flag requires 10 stars. If Suzanne can cut 5 stars in 20 minutes, how long will it take her to cut enough stars for 25 flags?

Discussion: This is another example of a problem that can be solved in several ways. Students can form a proportion as follows:

$$\frac{250}{x} = \frac{5}{20}$$

from which students will obtain 1,000 minutes, or 16 2/3 hours, or 16 hours and 40 minutes.

 Some students may recognize that Suzanne cuts the stars at a rate of 4 minutes per star (5 stars in 20 minutes). Furthermore, 25 flags require 250 stars. They can then multiply 250 by 4 minutes to obtain 1,000 minutes, or 16 hours 40 minutes.

Teacher's Notes:

ACTIVITY 27   **Title:**   "Rolling Fractions"

Purpose and Topic: This activity provides the opportunity for students to practice the four basic arithmetic operations using fractions with like and unlike denominators. It also offers the opportunity for the students to develop a strategy for building large and small fractions by adjusting their numerators and denominators appropriately.

Materials: A single die; 4 cards, each 3" × 5"; Reproduction Page 20

How to Make It: On each of the 3" × 5" cards, place one of the operations: +, −, ×, ÷. These are referred to as "Operation Cards." Give each student several copies of Reproduction Page 20, or have them draw their own similar game boards on a separate sheet of paper.

How to Use It: Follow these steps:

(a) The game is played by two students, each with a separate game board. Place the Operations Cards face down between the players. The students alternate turns deciding whether the game is to seek the greatest or smallest possible fraction. Once the student has announced "Greatest" or "Smallest," he or she picks the top Operations Card. This determines the sign that is placed in the circle between the fractions on the game board.

(b) The students alternate rolling the die. After the die is rolled, each player must put the number shown in the position he or she wishes on his or her own game board. The number cannot be moved during that game.

(c) After four rolls have been completed and the four numbers placed into position, each player finds the answer to his or her problem. The player who has the greatest (or smallest) answer gets 1 point.

(d) The players take a new game board and the game begins again. The first player to reach 5 points is the winner.

Here is a sample game:

Target: Smallest
Operations Card:

Number Rolled	Player #1	Player #2
4	$\frac{4}{\square} \ominus \frac{\square}{\square}$	$\frac{4}{\square} \ominus \frac{\square}{\square}$
3	$\frac{4}{\square} \ominus \frac{\square}{3}$	$\frac{4}{3} \ominus \frac{\square}{\square}$
4	$\frac{4}{\square} \ominus \frac{4}{3}$	$\frac{4}{3} \ominus \frac{4}{\square}$
6	$\frac{4}{6} \ominus \frac{4}{3}$	$\frac{4}{3} \ominus \frac{4}{6}$

Players now compute their answers. Player #1 will arrive at –2/3; player #2 will arrive at 2/3. Player #1 is the winner, since his fraction is smaller.

Problem 1: Jesse is the official team photographer for the Hornets football team. During the last quarter of their first game, he discovered that he had only 10 minutes of film left. Each play takes about 45 seconds. How many plays can Jesse shoot with his remaining film?

Discussion: Students should change 45 seconds to 3/4 of a minute, and then divide 10 minutes by 3/4. The result, 13 1/3 plays, is then stated as 13 plays. As an alternate solution, 10 × 60 = 600 seconds; 60 ÷ 45 = 13 1/3, or 13 plays.

Problem 2: The Robot Window Washing Corporation is putting on a demonstration at the new office building in town. The red robot began by washing 1/2 of the windows in the building. Then the blue robot washed 1/4 of the windows in the building. Next, the green robot washed 1/8 of the windows in the building. Finally, the yellow robot washed the remaining 5 windows. How many windows did each robot wash?

Discussion:

$$1/2 + 1/4 + 1/8 = 7/8$$
$$1 - 7/8 = 1/8$$

This $1/8 = 5$ windows; there must be 40 windows in the building. Then,

Red robot washes 1/2   = 20
Blue robot washes 1/4   = 10
Green robot washes 1/8   = 5
Yellow robot washes 1/8 = 5

An alternate solution might be as follows: Since the yellow robot washed 1/8 of the windows,

$$1/8 = 5 \text{ (yellow robot)}$$
$$1/8 = 5 \text{ (green robot)}$$
$$1/4 = 2/8 = 10 \text{ (blue robot)}$$
$$1/2 = 4/8 = 20 \text{ (red robot)}$$

Teacher's Notes:

ACTIVITY 28   **Title:** "Fraction Match-Up"

Purpose and Topic: This card game provides students with a wonderful opportunity to determine equivalent fractions, in both common and decimal form.

Materials: A deck of 3" × 5" cards

How to Make It: Prepare the deck of cards in sets of three. Each set contains three equivalent fractions, such as .15, 3/20, 18/120. There should be at least 10 similar sets, depending on the number of players. Here are 22 such sets:

1/2	1/4	3/4	3/8	5/8	7/8
6/12	5/20	36/48	21/56	56/40	21/24
.5	.25	.75	.375	.625	.875
1/5	2/5	3/5	4/5		
6/30	8/20	18/30	28/35		
.2	.4	.6	.8		
1/10	3/10	7/10	9/10	1/20	3/20
3/30	12/40	35/50	45/50	4/80	18/120
.1	.3	.7	.9	.05	.15
7/20	9/20	11/20	13/20	17/20	19/20
21/60	54/120	33/60	52/80	51/60	76/80
.35	.45	.55	.65	.85	.95

How to Use It: This game, which is for two to four players, is similar to Rummy. The deck is shuffled and the dealer is determined by each player drawing a card from the deck. The player who selects the largest fraction is the dealer. Six cards are dealt to each player, and the remaining cards are placed in a face-down pile (the "pack") in the center of the table. The game begins by the dealer turning the top card face up. The player to the dealer's left begins the play. He or she can pick up the face card or the top card from the pack. If the player now has three equivalent fractions, he places them in front of him and then discards one of the cards remaining in his hand, face up in the center. He now picks three cards from the pack to replace the ones he has placed in front of him. If the player does not have three equivalent fractions, he discards any card from his hand and play continues to the left. Players must always have six cards in their hands until the pack is used up. Play continues in this manner until the deck is exhausted or one player has no cards left. The winner is the person with the most sets of three in front of him or her.

Extension: This extension is played by three players and requires a deck of 30 cards (10 sets of 3). Shuffle the deck and deal the cards, one at a time, until each player has 10 cards. Players alternate turns placing one of their cards face up on the table. The player who completes a triple takes all the cards on the table at that time for his or her "bank." Play continues until no more triples are possible. The player with the most cards in his or her bank is the winner.

Problem 1:   In a drafting class, the assignment was to make a scale drawing of a 70-mile long road. Jen used a scale of 1 inch = 2 1/2 miles, whereas Wayne used a scale of 1 inch = 2.8 miles. Whose drawing of the road was larger? How much larger?

Discussion:

Jen: 70 ÷ 2 1/2 = 28 inches
Wayne: 70 ÷ 2.8   = 25 inches

Jen's line is 3 inches longer.

Problem 2:   Nancy, Oprah, and Penny live along the same straight road. Oprah lives between Nancy and Penny. Nancy lives 3 1/2 miles from Oprah and 5 3/4 miles from Penny. How far does Oprah live from Penny?

Discussion: Students should make a drawing.

5 3/4 − 3 1/2 = 2 1/4

Oprah lives 2 1/4 miles from Penny.

Teacher's Notes:

ACTIVITY 29   **Title:**   "Decimo"

Purpose and Topic: This game provides practice in reading decimals and understanding intuitive probability.

Materials: 20 small cards, each 1 1/2" × 1"; Reproduction Page 21

How to Make It: On each card, place one of the numerals from 0 through 9. Make two sets for each pair of players, a total of 20 cards.

How to Use It: Give each pair of students one deck of 20 cards and a copy of Reproduction Page 21 to serve as a game board. Each player draws a card from the top of the deck. The player with the higher number goes first, and play alternates. Return the two cards to the deck. Shuffle the deck of cards and place them face down between the players. Each player, in turn, draws the top card from the deck and places it anywhere he or she wishes on his or her own game board. This card cannot be moved (except as described below). Continue in this manner, placing numeral cards anywhere the player wishes in an empty square.
   If a player picks a card with 0, then he or she can do the following:

(a) Place the 0 on his or her game board in any empty square, or
(b) Switch the position of any 2 cards already on the game board (and discard the 0 card), or
(c) Move any one card on the game board to any empty square (and discard the 0 card).

When all five squares on the two game boards are filled, the player who has made the larger number is the winner of that round. Clear the game boards, replace all the cards, reshuffle the deck, and play again. The player who wins 2 out of 3 rounds is the winner of that game.

Extension: In order to give the game a little more spice, add three cards to the deck as follows:

(a) Move the decimal point one space to the left.
(b) Move the decimal point one space to the right.
(c) Move the decimal point two spaces to the right.

A player drawing one of these cards must follow the directions as stated.

Problem 1:   Martha can earn $5.00 an hour plus 50¢ for each doll she paints. Or she can receive $2.50 per hour, plus $1.05 for each doll she paints. She works 4 hours a day and paints 4 dolls an hour. Which is the better salary plan for Martha to choose?

Discussion: Students can figure the two salaries on a per hour base:

Plan #1:	4 dolls × 50¢	= $2.00
	hourly wage	= $5.00
		$7.00 per hour
Plan #2	4 dolls × $1.05	= $4.20
	hourly wage	= $2.50
		$6.70 per hour

Plan #1 is the better choice.

Problem 2:   The judges at the County Fair were weighing the giant vegetables. The eggplant weighed 10.4 pounds less than the giant watermelon. The watermelon was 2.2 pounds more than the giant squash. The squash weighed one-half as much as the pumpkin. The pumpkin won by weighing 36.8 pounds. How much did the four vegetables weigh together?

Discussion:

Pumpkin:	36.8
Squash:	18.4
Watermelon:	20.6
Eggplant:	10.2
	86.0

The four vegetables weighed 86 pounds together.

Teacher's Notes:

ACTIVITY 30   **Title:** "Decimal Tic-Tac-Toe"

Purpose and Topic: This game permits students to master changing common fractions into their equivalent decimal form.

Materials: Reproduction Page 22; fifteen 3" × 5" cards; tokens or some other material to cover items on the game board

How to Make It: Prepare a set of 15 cards, each with a common fraction on it, as shown here:

1/2	1/5	1/3	1/10	10/10
1/4	2/5	2/3	3/10	15/10
3/4	3/5		5/10	
	4/5		7/10	

Give each student a copy of Reproduction Page 22. List the decimal values on the board *without* their fraction equivalents. Students may select any nine of these decimals and write them randomly on their personal game board. Thus, for the set of fractions shown, the decimal equivalents would be:

1/2 = .5	1/5 = .2	1/3 = .333	1/10 = .1	10/10 = 1.0
1/4 = .25	2/5 = .4	2/3 = .667	3/10 = .3	15/10 = 1.5
3/4 = .75	3/5 = .6		5/10 = .5	
	4/5 = .8		7/10 = .7	

A typical game board might look like this:

.5	.1	.8
.7	.4	.3
.25	.2	.333

How to Use It: Shuffle the 15 fraction cards and place them in a stack, face down on your desk. Pick the top card from the pack and read it out loud. If a player has the decimal equivalent of the fraction read, he or she places a token or chip to cover it. Turn up the next card and read the fraction on it. Play continues until one student gets Tic-Tac-Toe (3 in a row, horizontally, vertically, or diagonally).

Extensions: The game can also be played in reverse, by having the students place the fractions on their game boards, while you read the decimal form. Play is the same as above. Another extension might be to include the percent equivalents in the game, and mix the numbers on the game boards as well as the cards.

Problem 1:   Al, Ben, and Charlie ordered a large pizza with mushrooms on 1/4 of it and olives on another 1/3 of it. The remainder of the pizza had anchovies. Al ate the part of the pizza that had only mushrooms. Ben ate the part of the pizza that had the olives. Charlie ate the part of the pizza with the anchovies. Who ate the most pizza, and how much did he eat?

Discussion: Convert each boy's share into fractions with a common denominator of 12:

     Al: 1/4 = 3/12
     Ben: 1/3 = 4/12

Therefore, Charlie ate the remaining 5/12 of the pizza.

Problem 2:   Five new crayons weigh the same as eight new pencils. If each pencil weighs 5.5 grams, how much does each new crayon weigh?

Discussion:

     1 pencil = 5.5 grams; 8 pencils = 44.0 grams
     44.0 grams ÷ 5 crayons = 8.8 grams per crayon

     Each crayon weighs 8.8 grams.

Teacher's Notes:

ACTIVITY 31   **Title:**   "Decimal Shape Drill"

Purpose and Topic: This activity presents a review and drill of decimal facts and operations. At the same time, it provides an opportunity for improving communication skills as students talk about geometric shapes.

Materials: Reproduction Pages 23 and 24; pencil and paper; a calculator

How to Make It: Give each student a copy of Reproduction Page 23. (You may wish to make an overhead transparency of the Reproduction Page in order to discuss it with the class). One student should be given the calculator. This student's job is to check any operations the other students perform.

How to Use It: Create a list of questions involving the numbers in the diagram. You might wish to discuss one or two of these to give the students the idea of the activity. Several sample questions follow (with the answers):

(a) Find the sum of the numbers that are in the rectangle but not in the circle or the triangle.
    (2.7 + 1.032 + .06 + 5.2 + 6.14 + .32 + .07 = 15.522)
(b) Find the largest number that is only in the square.   (1.01)
(c) What numbers are in the circle and the square, but not in the triangle?
    (.7, .02)
(d) What numbers are in the circle, the rectangle, and the triangle? What is their sum?   (2.56 + .037 + 1.09 + .015 = 3.702)
(e) What is the sum of the numbers that are only in the triangle? Which is the largest?   (.6 + 1.02 = 1.62)
(f) What is the sum of the numbers that are in the circle and the triangle, but not in the rectangle or the square?
    (5.72 + 1.6 + .72 + 2.06 + .005 = 10.105)
(g) What is the difference between the largest and smallest numbers that are in the circle but not in the triangle, rectangle, or square?
    (4.6 – .037 = 4.563)

Extensions: You might have the students prepare their own set of questions about the numbers in the figures. Or you may wish to use Reproduction Page 24 (which is the same configuration of shapes but is otherwise blank) to prepare a similar activity with fractions, whole numbers, integers, or a combination.

Problem 1: The maximum weight that an elevator can lift is 4,500 pounds. Each crate holds 58 boxes of stereo headphones, and each box weighs 11.85 pounds. What is the greatest number of crates the elevator can lift at one time?

Discussion:

$58 \times 11.85 = 687.3$ pounds
$4{,}500 \div 687.3 \approx 6.55$

The elevator can lift a maximum of 6 crates at a time.

Problem 2: Jerry works in the school store during the 6th period on Tuesdays. While he was working last week, he had 5 sales: $2.40, $1.00, $1.20, $1.25, $1.05. He also gave out change of 65¢ and 95¢. At the end of the 6th period, there was $13.65 in the cash box. How much was in the cash box at the start of the 6th period?

Discussion:

$2.40 + $1.00 + $1.20 + $1.25 + $1.05 = $6.90 total sales
$13.65 − $6.90 = $6.75

There was $6.75 in the cash box at the start of the period. (The change Jerry gave out is excess information.)

Teacher's Notes:

ACTIVITY 32   **Title:** "Percent Computer"

Purpose and Topic: This activity provides the student with a mechanical device for calculating all three cases of percent. The "computer" can be used to check the results of computation done by the traditional decimal, fraction, or proportion methods. Of course, readings will only be approximate.

Materials: Reproduction Page 25; a piece of string longer than line segment AB

How to Make It: Fasten the string to the top of the "computer" at point A, using a fastener, a piece of tape, or simply holding it in place with a finger.

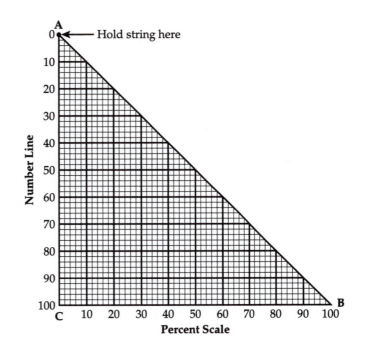

How to Use It: Follow these steps:

(a) *Using the computer to find: What is 40 percent of 50?*
Hold the string at point A. Stretch the string to cross BC at 40 (the percent). Read the answer where the string crosses the horizontal line at 50.

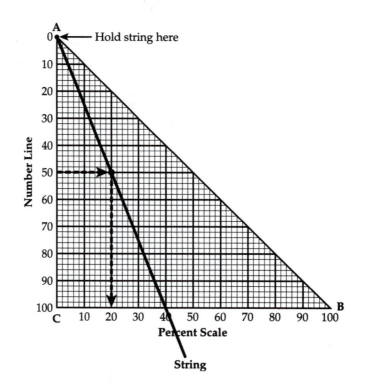

The coordinates of the point on the horizontal line are (20, 50). Thus, 40 percent of 50 is 20.

(b) *Using the computer to find: 6 is what percent of 30?*
Hold the string at point A. Locate the point whose coordinates are (6, 30). Stretch the string from point A through (6, 30) and extend it to cross line segment BC. It crosses this line at 20. Thus, 6 is 20 percent of 30.

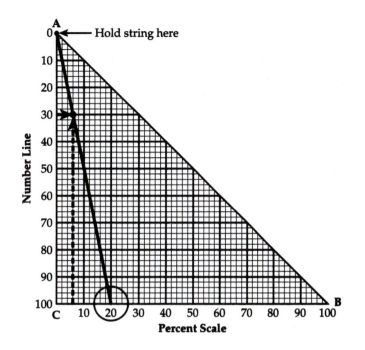

(c) *Using the computer to find: 12 is 30 percent of what number?*

Hold the string at point A. Stretch the string until it crosses line segment BC (the percent line) at 30. Locate the point where the string crosses the "12-line." The result is read on the number line (scale AC) as 40. Thus, 12 is 30 percent of 40.

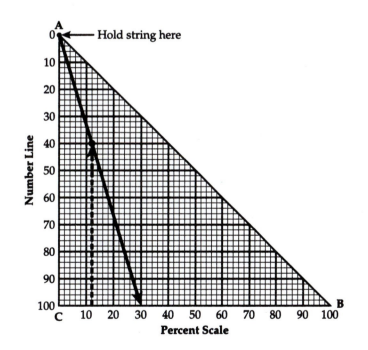

Here are some problems your students should solve with their Percent Computer and by any other method they know. Have them compare the answers they obtain. Discuss why the answers differ. (Students should realize that the Percent Computer yields only an approximate answer.)

Problem 1: Joe's Sporting Goods Emporium is having a sale—10 percent off on any piece of baseball equipment. Joanna bought a baseball glove whose original price was $35.00. How much did she pay for the glove?

Discussion:

$$10\% \times \$35.00 = \$3.50$$
$$\$35.00 - \$3.50 = \$31.50$$

Problem 2: Michael spent $12.60 for a year's subscription to *Kid's Computer Age* magazine. This represented a 60 percent savings on the newsstand price. What would the 12 issues have cost Michael if he had bought them on the newsstand?

Discussion: $12.60 represents 40 percent or 2/5 of the newsstand price, which must be $31.50.

Teacher's Notes:

CHAPTER THREE

Geometry

ACTIVITY 33 **Title:** "Angle Linkage"

Purpose and Topic: In courses in geometry, the basic figure most discussed is the angle. This model enables students to examine the dynamic properties of the angle.

Materials: Two pieces of poster-board or oak-tag, each 1/2" × 6"; a brass fastener; a protractor; a pair of scissors

How to Make It: Attach the two pieces of poster-board together at one end to form an angle.

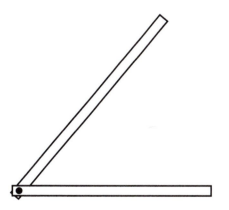

How to Use It: The model may be used to illustrate the different kinds of angles—acute, right, obtuse, and straight—by holding one side fixed and rotating the other side. Students should work in pairs. One student should

form angles of various sizes. The other student uses the protractor to measure the size of each angle.

Have the students fix an angle in place by tightening the brass fastener. The angle can contain any number of degrees. Have them measure the number of degrees in the angle with their protractors. Now tell them to cut off a piece from the open ends of one or both of the sides of the angle. Again, measure the number of degrees in the angle. Repeat this action several times, measuring the number of degrees in the angle after each cut. Students should realize that the number of degrees in the measure of an angle is not affected by the lengths of the sides.

Extension: Have one student challenge his or her partner to form an angle of a given number of degrees. The angle should then be measured with a protractor to determine the accuracy of the angle. Reverse roles and repeat the action. This will help the students enhance their skills at estimating angles.

Problem 1:   At the class picnic, Stan spent his 8-hour day as follows:

2 hours playing softball
1 hour rowing on the lake
1 hour for lunch
2 hours playing tennis
1 hour at the sack races
1 hour at horseshoes

Show this information on a circle graph.

Discussion: The circle graph contains 360°. Since this is an 8-hour day, each hour will contain 45°.

Problem 2:   Donna was asked to divide an obtuse angle into four equal parts. The sum of two resulting angle measures was 60°. What was the measure of the original obtuse angle?

Discussion: Since two of the equal angles contain a total of 60°, each must contain 30°. The original angle contained 4 × 30°, or 120°.

Teacher's Notes:

ACTIVITY 34   **Title:** "Curve Stitching"

Purpose and Topic: This activity provides an opportunity for students to produce some esthetically pleasing designs using some of the techniques of geometry.

Materials: Rulers; protractors; compasses; poster-board; needles; embroidery thread

How to Use It: Provide each student with some brightly colored embroidery thread, an embroidery needle, and a piece of poster-board to serve as background. The color of the thread should not be the same as that of the poster-board. Have them begin by drawing a pair of lines that meet at about a 45° angle. To create the design, have them use their rulers or compasses to mark 10 equally spaced arcs on each ray of the angle. Label the intersections from 1 through 10 on each ray, as shown here:

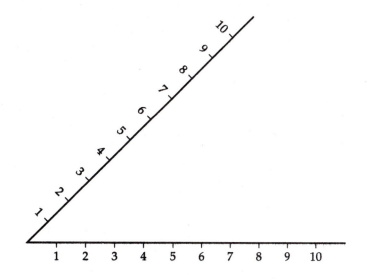

To create this design, students connect numbers on each ray whose sum is 11 (i.e., 1 to 10, 2 to 9, 3 to 8, etc.). The finished design looks like this:

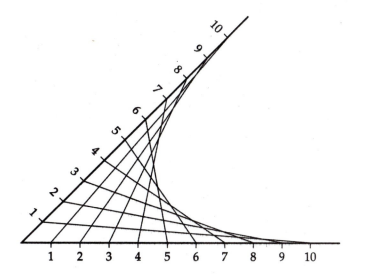

The design can be extended by using supplementary angles as axes, as shown here:

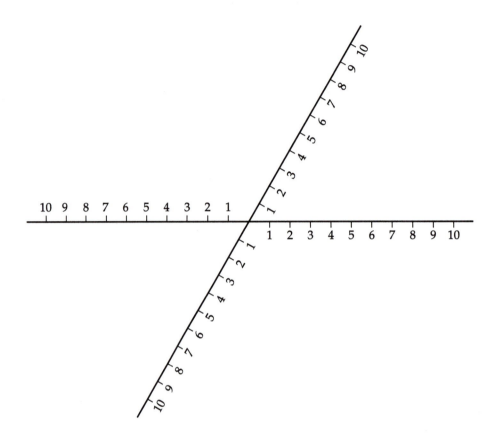

To make the design, have the students connect points on the axes in each region whose sum is 11, as shown here:

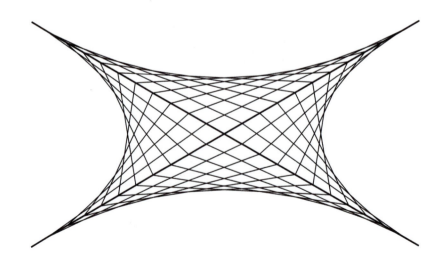

To make their design about a common point (as shown here), have the students draw rays that meet to form six 60° angles.

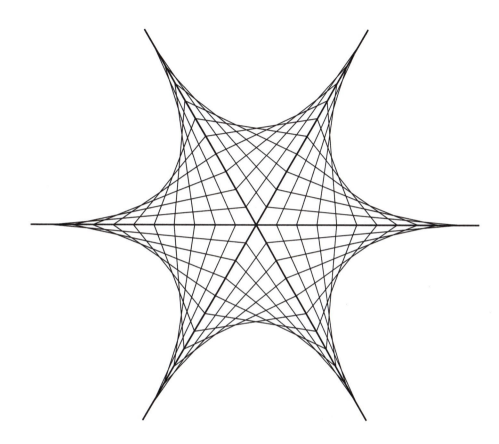

Permit the students to create their own designs (or combinations of designs). These will form an excellent class exhibit.

Extensions: Have the students begin by drawing a circle rather than an angle. Divide the circumference of the circle into 36 equally spaced points, labeled from 1 through 36. Join 1 to 2, 2 to 4, 3 to 6 ... n to $2n$ (or n to $2n - 36$ once they reach 19). The finished stitching will yield the *cardioid*. Similarly, beginning with the circle and connecting 1 to 3, 2 to 6, 3 to 9, ... n to $3n$ (or $3n - 36$, once they reach $n = 12$) will yield the curve known as the *nephroid*.

Problem: An artist created a curve stitching sculpture by using two rays forming a 90° angle and marking 10 points on each ray. However, she used wire instead of thread and welded the points of intersection of the wires. How many points did she weld?

Discussion: One possible solution is to actually do the art project and count the points of intersection. However, by reducing the number of points on each axis to 1, and then expanding the number of points to 2, then 3, and so on, a pattern emerges:

Number of Points on Each Axis	Number of Welds
1	0
2	1
3	3
4	6
5	10
•	•
•	•
•	•
10	45

These are the triangular numbers, and for 10 points, the total number of welds would be 45.

Some students may recognize that the general formula for this pattern is:

$$\frac{n\,(n-1)}{2}$$

Teacher's Notes:

ACTIVITY 35   **Title:** "Straws and Triangles"

Purpose and Topic: A property of triangles is that the sum of the lengths of two sides must always be greater than the third side. In this activity, students will attempt to construct triangles, given an assortment of different lengths to be used as sides. They will discover the property under consideration.

Materials: Straws; Reproduction Page 26

How to Make It: Prepare five lengths of straws for each student or group of students: 1", 1 1/2", 2", 2 1/2", and 3". Label the pieces (a) through (e), respectively. Give each student a copy of Reproduction Page 26.

How to Use It: Divide the class into groups of four students. Give each group a packet of the five straws, cut into the appropriate lengths as just indicated. Each student should have a copy of Reproduction Page 26. Have the groups pick any three straws and attempt to form a triangle. Record their results in the table. (Two examples have already been done.) Repeat this action until all 10 possible combinations have been attempted and discussed. The completed table should appear as follows:

Pieces	Lengths			Can a Triangle Be Formed?
	Side 1	*Side 2*	*Side 3*	
a, b, c	1"	1 1/2"	2"	Yes
a, b, d	1"	1 1/2"	2 1/2"	No
a, b, e	1"	1 1/2"	3"	No
a, c, d	1"	2"	2 1/2"	Yes
a, c, e	1"	2"	3"	No
a, d, e	1"	2 1/2"	3"	Yes
b, c, d	1 1/2"	2"	2 1/2"	Yes
b, c, e	1 1/2"	2"	3"	Yes
b, d, e	1 1/2"	2 1/2"	3"	Yes
c, d, e	2"	2 1/2"	3"	Yes

Help the students conclude that the sum of the lengths of two sides of any triangle must be greater than the length of the third side.

Extensions: Try the following modifications:

  (a) Discuss the relationship between the size of the angles and the lengths of the sides opposite these angles. (The longest side lies opposite the largest angle; the shortest side lies opposite the smallest angle.)
  (b) Give each group of students 12 Popsicle sticks, straws, stirrers, and so on, all the same length. Using all 12 each time, have the students make and describe all the different triangles they can form. A logical approach would be to form a table beginning with 1-1-10, 1-2-9, 1-3-8, and so on, noting which ones form triangles. There are three: 4-4-4 (equilateral); 3-4-5 (right); and 5-5-2 (isosceles).

Problem 1:   The following advertisement appeared in a local newspaper:

LAND FOR SALE ! ! !

A plot of land in the shape of a right triangle whose sides are 30 yards, 60 yards, and 90 yards is offered for sale at $150 per square yard. Interested parties should call 555-5555.

How much should you spend for this plot of land?

Discussion: No such triangular plot of land could exist, since $30 + 60 = 90$. Thus, you should spend $0 for this plot of land. (Many students will go ahead and calculate the area as $(1/2)(30)(60) = 900$ square yards.)

Problem 2:   A sculptor has two copper triangles, each a right triangle whose sides are 3', 4', and 5'. She welds the triangles together into a single figure by joining two congruent sides. What is the perimeter of the new figure?

Discussion: There are actually three possible answers, depending on which sides are joined. If the sculptor joins the 3' sides, the resulting triangle has a perimeter of 18'. If she joins the 4' sides, the resulting triangle has a perimeter of 16'. If she joins the 5' sides, she will have a quadrilateral whose perimeter is 14'.

Teacher's Notes:

ACTIVITY 36   **Title:**   "Sum of the Interior Angles of a Triangle"

Purpose and Topic: This activity will help students discover that the sum of the measures of the interior angles of any triangle is 180 degrees.

Materials: Triangles of varying size and shape cut from construction paper

How to Make It: Cut a set of acute triangles, obtuse triangles, and right triangles from construction paper. The shapes of the triangles should vary as much as possible.

How to Use It: Give every student a triangle. Have them tear off the three angles as shown here:

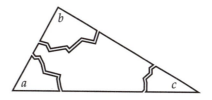

Have the students place the three angles so that they are adjacent and have their vertices meeting at a common point. Ask them to tell what they notice about the sum of the three angles of their respective triangles.

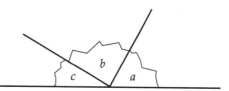

Have them check their results with a protractor.

Extension: Have your students draw any triangle on a sheet of paper. Form the exterior angles by extending one side at each vertex. Tell them to cut out the three exterior angles and place them so that they are adjacent and their vertices meet at a common point. What do the students discover? The three angles should form a region about the point which contains 360°. (*Note:* The students should measure their three angles with a protractor to verify that the sum is indeed 360°. This is true regardless of the triangle drawn.)

Problem 1:   Stan and Roz were arguing about the number of degrees in angle *x* of the following figure:

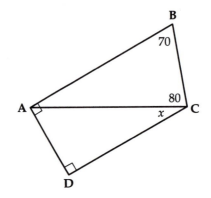

Roz felt that it had to be 10°, since ∠A and ∠D were both right angles and therefore the measure of angle BCD had to be 90° as well. Stan felt that this was not right, since ∠D contained 90°, and, if ∠x contained 10°, then ∠CAD must contain 80°, "and it sure doesn't look it," he said. How many degrees do you think there are in angle ACD?

Discussion: The number of degrees in the measure of angle CAB is 180 − (70 + 80) = 30°. Thus, the measure of angle CAD = 60°, and ∠x contains [180 − (90 + 60)] = 30°.

Problem 2:   A kite is made up of two isosceles triangular sheets of paper on a common base, as shown here:

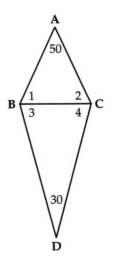

The vertex angle of the smaller triangle contains 50°, whereas the vertex angle of the larger triangle contains 30°. Find the number of degrees in each of the other two angles of the kite.

Discussion: The solution to this problem depends on the fact that the angles opposite the equal sides of an isosceles triangle have the same measure. Thus, $\angle 1 = \angle 2$ and $\angle 3 = \angle 4$. Since the sum of the angles of a triangle is 180°, $\angle 1 + \angle 2$ contains 130°, or each contains 65°. Similarly, $\angle 3$ and $\angle 4$ each contain 75°. Angle ABD = 65° + 75° = 140°, the same as angle ACD.

Problem 3: Mark measured the three exterior angles of his triangle and discovered that the number of degrees in the angles were in the ratio 3:4:5. How many degrees are there in each interior angle of the triangle?

Discussion: An algebraic solution yields:

$$3x + 4x + 5x = 360°$$
$$12x = 360°$$
$$x = 30°$$

The exterior angles contain 90° (3 × 30), 120° (4 × 30), and 150° (5 × 30). The interior angles will contain 90°, 60°, and 30°, respectively.

Those students with little background in algebra can solve the problem by using the guess and test strategy. That is, the ratio of 3:4:5 suggests 30°, 40°, 50°, which sums to only 120°. Since the sum is to be 360°, they should then multiply each guess by 3.

Teacher's Notes:

ACTIVITY 37   **Title:**   "Sum of the Interior Angles of a Convex Polygon"

Purpose and Topic: This activity leads to the generalization that the sum of the interior angles of any n-sided, convex polygon is $(n-2)$ straight angles or $(n-2)180°$.

Materials: Paper; pencil; ruler; Reproduction Page 27

How to Make It: Have students draw several convex polygons, each with a different number of sides, from 3 through 8.

How to Use It: Each student should divide their set of polygons into adjacent triangles, by selecting any vertex and drawing all of the diagonals from that vertex, as shown here:

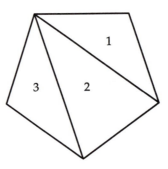

Use Reproduction Page 27 to fill in the table. Students should conclude that the sum of the interior angles of any n-sided polygon is $(n-2)180°$.

Extensions: Each student, or group of students, should draw any quadrilateral or any other convex polygon. (A pentagon is used here for illustrative purposes.) Have students extend each side to form an exterior angle at each vertex.

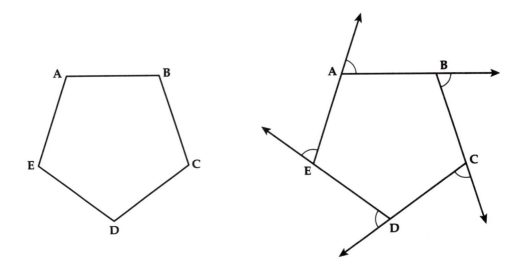

Carefully use the protractor to measure each exterior angle. Find the sum of the exterior angles for each figure they have drawn. The students should conclude that, regardless of the number of sides, the sum of the exterior angles of any convex polygon will be 360°.

Another approach would be to have the students cut out the exterior angles of a convex polygon and place them about a point. They will form a figure containing 360°.

Problem 1:   The students in the seventh grade are enclosing a plot for the class garden. The plot is in the shape of a quadrilateral with three consecutive interior angles measuring 90°, 80°, and 110°. What is the measure of the fourth angle?

Discussion: The sum of the interior angles of a quadrilateral is 360°. The sum of the three given angles is 280°. The fourth angle contains 80°.

Problem 2:   The Lopez family is going camping! They are setting up their tent, the base of which is in the shape of a pentagon with all sides and angles equal. They are driving the pegs into the ground at each vertex. What is the angle they must use between each adjacent pair of sides?

Discussion: The sum of the interior angles of a pentagon is found as follows:

$$(n - 2)180°$$
$$(5 - 2)180°$$
$$(3)180° = 540°$$

Since all five angles are equal, each must contain 108°.

Teacher's Notes:

ACTIVITY 38   **Title:** "Building Rectangles"

Purpose and Topic: The students will discover that, if the diagonals of a quadrilateral are congruent and bisect each other, then the quadrilateral must be a rectangle (necessary and sufficient conditions).

Materials: 2 strips of poster-board, each 1/4" × 4"; one brass fastener

How to Make It: Punch a hole at the midpoint of each strip. Fasten them together with the fastener. Place a mark at the center of the top and bottom edges of each strip.

How to Use It: Have the students open the two fastened strips as much as they wish. Lay the device on a piece of paper and mark a point at the extreme edges of each strip where the mark has been made. Remove the strips and draw straight lines connecting the four points. Ask the students to describe what figure they have obtained. Use a protractor and a ruler to have them check their results. Repeat the experiment several times. (*Note:* Some students may make the diagonals perpendicular, and thus form a square.) Students may be surprised that the only figure they can obtain is a rectangle.

Extension: Have the students punch holes and fasten the diagonals at any point other than the midpoint (e.g., at the one-third point on each strip). An isosceles trapezoid will result. Have them experiment with different positions of the fastener on each strip.

Problem 1:   Mrs. Johnson, the sponsor of the Garden Club, divided her club members into three groups of seven students. She gave each group 100 feet of rope, and told them to go into the local field and lay out a rectangular plot of land using the rope. They then were told to measure the length and width of their group's plot. To their surprise, each group had a different area. Group A had a plot of 400 square feet, Group B had a plot of 600 square feet, and Group C had a plot of 525 square feet. Yet all of the groups had used the same amount of rope (100 feet) to build their rectangles.

(a) How did this happen?
(b) What would be the maximum area they could have enclosed?

Discussion: The students should realize that the area of a rectangle can vary, even though the perimeter remains a constant. A table easily reveals this:

Length	Width	Area	Perimeter
40	10	400	100
35	15	525	100
30	20	600	100
25	25	625	100
20	30	600	100

Problem 2:   Rhoda is making a quilt for the crafts fair. The quilt is rectangular, with a length of 108" and a width of 72". She wants to sew ribbon around the entire border. If the ribbon costs 25¢ per foot, how much will Rhoda spend for the ribbon?

Discussion: The perimeter of the rectangular quilt is 2 (108) + 2 (72) = 360 inches, or 30 feet. At 25¢ per foot, the ribbon will cost Rhoda $7.50.

Teacher's Notes:

ACTIVITY 39   **Title:** "Building Parallelograms"

Purpose and Topic: Students will discover that, if the diagonals of a quadrilateral are not congruent (i.e., they are unequal in length) but bisect each other, then the quadrilateral must be a parallelogram.

Materials: 2 strips of poster-board of different lengths, each 1/4" thick; one brass fastener; Reproduction Page 28 (for Problem 2)

How to Make It: Punch a hole at the midpoint of each strip. Fasten them together with the fastener. Place a mark at the center of the top and bottom of each strip.

How to Use It: Have the students open the two fastened strips as much as they wish. Lay the device on a piece of paper and mark a point at the extreme edges of each strip. Remove the strips and draw straight lines connecting the four points. Ask the students to describe what figure they have obtained. Use a ruler to have them check their results. Repeat the experiment several times. (*Note:* Some students may make the diagonals perpendicular, and thus form a rhombus.) Students may be surprised that the only figure they can obtain is a parallelogram.

Extension: Have the students use a ruler and a protractor to discover some of the properties of a parallelogram:

   (a) The opposite angles are congruent (have the same measure).
   (b) The opposite sides are congruent (have the same measure).
   (c) The consecutive angles are supplementary (their angle sum = 180°).

Initiate a discussion to have the students discover that, if the diagonals of the parallelogram are perpendicular, then the parallelogram is a rhombus.

Problem 1: Mrs. Marinello just bought a wallpaper border for her den. The design shows 8 squares in a row, arranged so that squares next to each other share a full side. Each side of the square is 10 inches long. What is the perimeter of the design?

Discussion: Have the students make a drawing. The design will be 8 units long by 1 unit wide. Its perimeter will be 18 units, or 180 inches long.

Problem 2: For this problem, provide each student with a copy of Reproduction Page 28. Have them cut out the four rhombus tiles shown. Tell the students to form different figures using the four tiles. Tiles may meet at a vertex. However, if sides are common, they must coincide completely. What is the maximum perimeter they can form? What is the minimum perimeter they can form?

Discussion: Perimeters will vary with the figure drawn. The maximum perimeter will be 32" and the minimum perimeter will be 16".

Teacher's Notes:

ACTIVITY 40   **Title:**   "Area of Parallelograms and Triangles"

Purpose and Topic: Students are often presented with a series of formulas for the areas of various plane figures such as the rectangle, parallelogram, and triangle. Although they memorize the formulas, they often do not really understand how they were developed. This activity provides a physical model that relates the areas of these figures in a way that is easily understood.

Materials: Unit squares (cut from cardboard or made from paper); grid paper; plain paper; ruler; scissors; tape

How to Make It: Have each student cut a nonrectangular parallelogram from the grid paper. Have them also cut two congruent triangles from the plane paper. (*Note:* Individual students may decide to make their triangles obtuse, right, or acute. There are no restrictions.) Put these aside temporarily.

How to Use It: Follow these steps:

(a) To develop the formula for the area of a rectangle, have each student take 12 of the unit squares and create several different rectangles (1 × 12, 2 × 6, 3 × 4). Find the area of each by counting the number of unit squares. The area of each is 12 square units. Show that the area of each rectangle is its base multiplied by its height, $b \times h$ (or length × width).

(b) Now have students take the parallelograms they have cut from the grid paper. Tell them to draw the altitude from one vertex and cut out the right triangle thus formed. Place this triangle on the other side of the parallelogram to form a rectangle, as shown here:

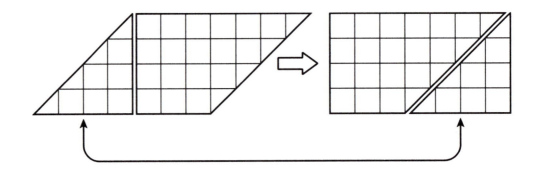

Help the students discover that the base of their parallelogram is still b, and the height is still h. Since all they have done is reconfigure the original rectangle, the area of their parallelogram is also $b \times h$.

(c) Have the students take the pair of congruent triangles they have cut from the plain paper. Tell them to draw the altitude. Start with one triangle placed on top of the other. Now move one triangle and place it so that a pair of corresponding sides coincide. The resulting figure will be a parallelogram, as shown here:

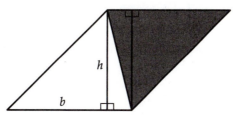

Since the base of parallelogram is b and its altitude or height is h, the area is $b \times h$. But the parallelogram is made up of the two congruent triangles. Thus, the area of each triangle is one-half the area of the parallelogram, or $(1/2)(b \times h)$.

Extension: To find the area of a trapezoid, have the students cut two congruent trapezoids from paper. Discuss the dimensions of each one. The parallel sides are called the bases, (b and b'), whereas the height (h) is the distance between the two bases. Starting with the parallelograms placed on top of one another, move one of them so that a pair of corresponding, non-parallel sides coincide, as follows:

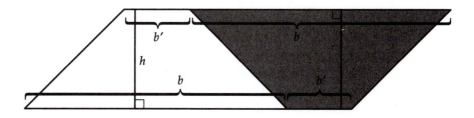

The result is, again, a parallelogram. The base of the parallelogram is $(b + b')$, whereas the height is h. Thus, the area of each trapezoid is one-half that of the parallelogram, or $(1/2)(b + b')(h)$.

Problem 1:   Two square mats, each 8 inches on a side, are placed as shown:

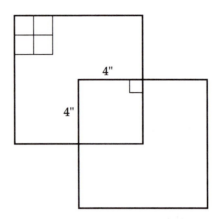

The resulting figure is to be covered with small, 1" square tiles. (The first 4 have already been placed). How many of these 1" square tiles are needed?

Discussion: The area of the total figure is the area of the two large squares minus the area of overlap, which is also a square. Thus, you obtain $8 \times 8 = 64$ for the area of one large square, or 128 for the two. The smaller square has an area of 16. Thus, the number of small squares needed is $128 - 16 = 112$.

Problem 2:   Mr. Wilson, a local contractor, has been hired to build a walkway around a swimming pool. The walkway, which is to be 3' wide, will be made from 1' square ceramic tiles. The pool is rectangular, 60' long by 30' wide. How many tiles does Mr. Wilson need?

Discussion: A drawing will reveal that, just considering the perimeter of the pool, there will be 9 square feet of tile missing in each corner. Thus, Mr. Wilson needs:

$60 \times 3 = 180$ tiles for each length = 360
$30 \times 3 = 90$ tiles for each width = 180
$4 \times 9 = 36$ tiles for the corners = 36

Mr. Wilson needs a total of 576 tiles.

Teacher's Notes:

ACTIVITY 41   **Title:** "Tangrams"

Purpose and Topic: Tangrams are one of the oldest puzzles known. They have been used for many years, especially in the Far East. They provide an excellent opportunity for students to use their creativity and imagination as well as to work with area and perimeter formulas. (For additional activities with tangrams, see Activity 24.)

Materials: Reproduction Page 29; scissors

How to Make It: Give each student a copy of Reproduction Page 29. Have all students cut out their own set of tangrams. (For a more permanent set of tangram pieces, duplicate the tangrams onto a sheet of light cardboard or oak-tag.)

How to Use It: Follow these steps:

(a) Discuss how the tangram set was developed. That is, points E and F are midpoints of sides AD and CD, respectively. Point G is the intersection of the two diagonals of the original square ABCD; point H is the midpoint of segment EF; point J is the midpoint of segment CG; and point I is the midpoint of segment AG.

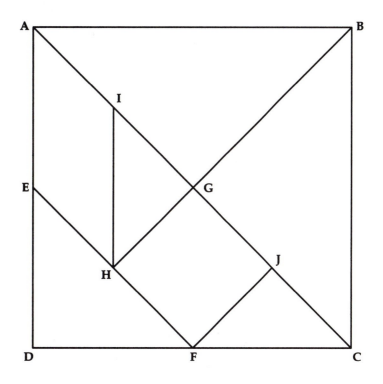

(b) Have the students put the seven pieces back into the original square shape shown in the figure. Challenge them to make a nonsquare rectangle by moving exactly two of the pieces. Ask a student to demonstrate his or her results.

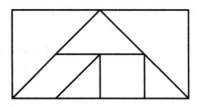

(c) Now have them move just one piece and change the rectangle into a parallelogram. Again, have a student demonstrate his or her results.

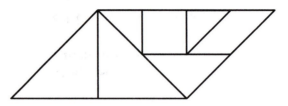

(d) Now have the students move just one piece and change the parallelogram into a trapezoid.

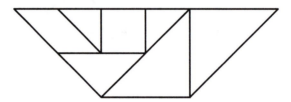

(e) Assume that one side of the original square is exactly 4 inches in length.

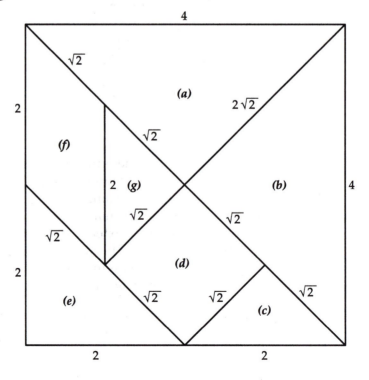

What would be the area of each of the seven tangram pieces?

Figure	Perimeter	Area
(a)	$4 + 4\sqrt{2}$	4
(b)	$4 + 4\sqrt{2}$	4
(c)	$2 + 2\sqrt{2}$	1
(d)	$4\sqrt{2}$	2
(e)	$4 + 2\sqrt{2}$	2
(f)	$4 + 2\sqrt{2}$	2
(g)	$2 + 2\sqrt{2}$	1

Extensions: Have students use their seven-piece set of tangrams to make figures similar to those shown here:

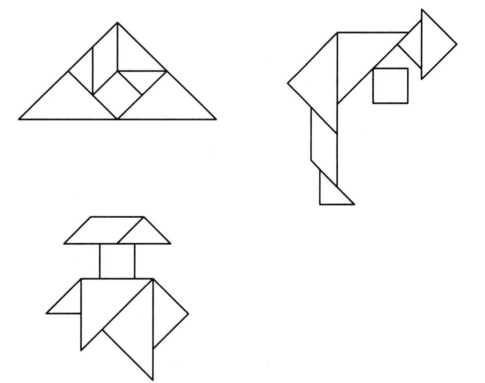

Then have them trace the outline of their figures and exchange them with a neighbor. See if the students can duplicate the original figures. Remember that all seven pieces of the tangrams must be used in each creation, thus the area of each figure will remain constant.

This activity can be extended to include determining the perimeter of each of the seven pieces. This depends on the students having a knowledge of the Pythagorean theorem (included in the dimensions in the figure above and in the perimeters above).

Teacher's Notes:

ACTIVITY 42   **Title:** "Find Me!"

Purpose and Topic: This activity provides students with an opportunity to recognize various polygons.

Materials: Reproduction Page 30; colored markers

How To Use It: Provide each student with a copy of Reproduction Page 30 and a marker. Have the students shade at least one of each of the required shapes on the accompanying grid, and place the letter of the polygon inside the figure they have shaded. For example, three shapes are shaded here:

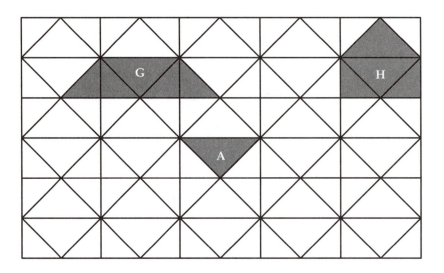

When the students are finished, prepare a transparency of the grid for the overhead projector. Have different students come to the overhead and outline their shapes. Discuss the properties of each shape and show them on the figure.

Extension: The same grid can be used to find more restrictive shapes, such as an isosceles trapezoid, a trapezoid with a right angle, an isosceles right triangle, and so on.

Problem 1: Two 6" × 6" squares are placed side by side to form a rectangle. A 6" × 8" rectangle is then painted on the original figure. What is the area of the nonpainted portion?

Discussion: The answer is independent of where the rectangle is painted. In any case, the unpainted area will be (12 × 6) – (8 × 6) or 72 – 48 = 24 square inches.

Problem 2:   A square sheet of paper, 8" × 8", is folded in half to form a rectangle. The rectangle is then folded in half. What is the perimeter of the final figure?

Discussion: The first time the paper is folded, it forms a rectangle whose sides are 8" × 4". The second time it is folded, however, there can be two results, depending on the way in which the second fold is made. If you fold the paper in the same direction as before, you obtain a rectangle with dimensions 8" × 2" and a perimeter of 20". If you make the second fold perpendicular to the original fold, you obtain a square with dimensions 4" × 4" and a perimeter of 16".

Teacher's Notes:

ACTIVITY 43   **Title:** "Geominos"

Purpose and Topic: This activity provides students with practice in recognizing the properties of geometric figures.

Materials: 28 small geomino cards

How to Make It: The six geometric shapes used in this game are the triangle, circle, square, rectangle, parallelogram, and trapezoid. Each shape is represented by a defining property. (Of course, a single property can be associated with more than one shape.) The geominoes appear on Reproduction Page 31. They can be cut out as shown, pasted onto oak-tag or poster-board before cutting, or simply copied onto a set of cards.

How to Use It: The game can be played by two to four students. The set of geominos are placed face down on the table. One player is designated as the dealer; he or she distributes six geominos to each player. Beginning with the dealer, the first player who has a "double" begins play by placing the double face up on the board. If no one has a double, players take turns picking another geomino from the table until a double appears. The first player who picks a double begins play by placing the double face up on the board. (*Note:* Some "doubles" consist of a figure and its defining property; for example, the geomino that shows a triangle and the property "it has exactly three sides" is a double.) Play continues as in ordinary dominoes. A "train" is built by placing matching figures adjacently. Either a figure or a property description of that figure can be used as a match.

   If the player in turn cannot match either end of the "train" with the geominos in his or her hand, then that player picks from the pile of remaining geominos until a match is obtained. The winner is the first player who uses up all his or her geominos, or the player with the fewest geominos remaining when there are no further matches.

Extensions: The game can be extended to include other figures and their properties. It can also be extended to include 3-dimensional figures.

Problem 1:   How much smaller is the area of a rectangular field 80' × 50' than the area of a square field with the same perimeter?

Discussion: The perimeter of the rectangular field is 260'. Therefore, each side of the square field is 65'. The area of the square field is 65 × 65 or 4225 square feet, whereas the area of the rectangular field is 80 × 50 or 4000 square feet. The rectangular field is 225 square feet smaller than the square field.

Problem 2: How many 3" × 6" dominoes are needed to cover a square board that is 3' on each side?

Discussion: Since 3 and 6 are each factors of 36 (3' = 36"), the dominoes will fit exactly, whether placed horizontally or vertically. The area of a domino is 18 square inches, whereas the area of the board is 1,296 square inches. It will require 72 dominoes to cover the board.

Some students may reason that they will need 6 of the 6" side placed along the 36" side of the board, and there will be 12 of the 3" side. They need 12 x 6 or 72 dominoes to cover the board.

An interesting extension would be to have students construct a set of dominoes 6" x 3" and a square board that is 3' on each side. Let them discover different ways to place the dominoes on the board to cover it.

Teacher's Notes:

ACTIVITY 44   **Title:** "Geometry Concentration"

Purpose and and Topic: Students will identify basic geometric figures and their defining, basic properties.

Materials: A deck of 24 index cards (3" × 5"); Reproduction Page 32

How to Make It: Reproduction Page 32 shows the 24 cards used in the game. If you wish to make a permanent deck, copy these figures and the associated names on 3" × 5" cards. Otherwise, simply have the students cut out the 24 cards to make a deck.

How to Use It: Each competing group of two, three, or four players uses one deck. One player is designated as the dealer. He or she shuffles the deck and deals the cards, face down, into a 4 × 6 array in the center of the playing area. This player turns over any two cards. If they match, he or she removes the two cards from the array and takes another turn. If the cards do not match, they are turned back face down in their original position on the board. The next player takes a turn. The game ends when the board is cleared. The winner is the player who has taken the most cards at the end of the game.

Problem 1:   The following figure shows a triangle with angles as marked. Find the number of degrees in each of the angles marked *a, b, c,* and *d*.

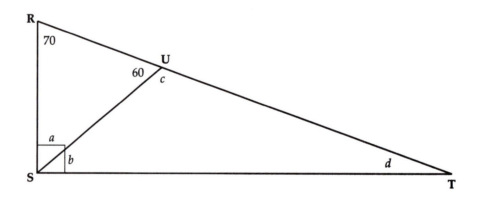

Discussion: Since this is a right triangle and angle SRT contains 70°, angle *d* must contain 20°. Using the fact that the sum of the measures of the angles of a triangle is 180°, the measure of angle *a* is 50°, the measure of angle *b* is 40°, and the measure of angle *c* is 120°.

Problem 2: Given a rectangle, which yields the greater area:

- **(a)** Increase the length by 40 percent and decrease the width by 20 percent, or
- **(b)** Decrease the length by 20 percent and increase the width by 40 percent?

Discussion: Let l and w represent the length and width of the original rectangle. Then:

- **(a)** $1.4\,l \times .8\,w = (1.4)(.8)(l)(w)$
- **(b)** $.8\,l \times 1.4\,w = (.8)(1.4)(l)(w)$

By the commutative principle, these two expressions are the same. There is no difference in the areas.

Students with little algebra at their command can assign dimensions to the rectangle. For example, begin with a rectangle that is $100'' \times 60''$. Then:

- **(a)** $1.40\,l \times .48\,w = .672\,lw$
- **(b)** $.80\,l \times .84\,w = .672\,lw$

Again, the areas are the same.

Teacher's Notes:

ACTIVITY 45   **Title:**   "Must Be . . . Can Be"

Purpose and Topic: This game is designed to provide students with a review of the properties of selected geometric figures. In addition, they will encounter the concept of *necessary* (must have) as opposed to *sufficient* (can have).

Materials: Twenty-eight 3" × 5" index cards for each group of players

How to Make It: The game requires two sets of cards: 8 Figure Cards and 20 Property Cards. Copy each of the Figure Card names and Property Card statements shown below on a separate card.

Figure Cards

(1) Right triangle	**(4)** Square	**(7)** Rhombus
(2) Rectangle	**(5)** Obtuse triangle	**(8)** Triangle
(3) Parallelogram	**(6)** Isosceles trapezoid	

Property Cards

	(Answers)
(a) My consecutive angles are supplementary.	2, 3, 4, 7
(b) Two of my three angles are complementary.	1
(c) The sum of the measures of two of my three angles is less than 90°.	5
(d) My two diagonals are congruent but not perpendicular.	2, 4, 6
(e) The formula for my area is $A = (1/2)(b + b')$.	6
(f) Exactly one pair of my opposite sides are parallel.	6
(g) Either of my two diagonals divides me into two isosceles triangles.	4, 7
(h) Either of my two diagonals divides me into two congruent triangles.	2, 3, 4, 7
(i) My four sides are congruent but my four angles are not.	7
(j) My four angles are congruent and my two diagonals are also congruent.	2, 4
(k) Any one of my angles is supplementary to each of the other three.	2, 4
(l) My two diagonals are perpendicular and bisect each other.	4, 7
(m) My two diagonals are not congruent but bisect each other.	3, 7
(n) The formula for my area is $A = (1/2)(b)(h)$.	1, 5, 8
(o) Each of my four sides has the same measure.	4, 7
(p) My opposite sides are congruent but my adjacent sides are not.	2, 3
(q) My four sides are congruent but my diagonals are not.	7

(r) Either of my two diagonals divide me into two congruent right triangles.   2, 4

(s) The sum of the measures of my angles is 180°.   1, 5, 8

(t) No more than two of my angles are acute angles.   1, 5

How to Use It: Each competing group of two, three, or four players uses one Figure Deck and one Property Deck. Players shuffle the two decks separately. The Figure Deck is placed face down in a single pile, and the Property Deck is dealt face down on the table between the players, into a 4 × 5 card array. The first player turns over the top Figure Card, and then turns over any card from the array of Property Cards, in an attempt to match the property with the figure. If the Property Card is a property of the figure, then the player takes the Property Card and places it in front of him or her. The Figure Card is then placed at the bottom of the Figure Card deck. If it is not a property of that figure, then the Property Card is replaced face down in its original position in the array, and the Figure Card is placed at the bottom of the Figure Card deck. (It will obviously reappear later on.) Play continues until all the Property Cards have been removed. The winner is the player who has the most Property Cards at the end of the game.

Notice that the Property Cards may apply to more than one figure and can be "matched" several times. For example, the property "My diagonal divides me into two congruent triangles" is a property of a parallelogram, a square, a rectangle, and a rhombus. On the other hand, suppose the Property Card reads, "Two of my three angles are complementary." This must be true for the right triangle, but it is not a general property of a triangle. Thus, this property matches only the right triangle.

Problem 1: In the parallelogram shown here, the dimensions are as given. Can you find the perimeter and the area of the parallelogram? Why or why not?

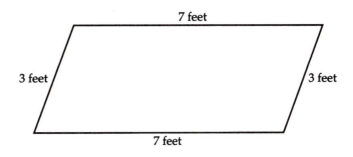

Discussion: The altitude of the parallelogram has not been given. The area cannot be determined. However, the perimeter is 20 feet.

Problem 2:   Priscilla is roping off an area for her company's plot at the flower show. She has 48' of rope to mark off the area.

- **(a)** Can she make a rectangular plot with an area of 140 square feet?
- **(b)** What is the rectangle of maximum area she can create using all of her rope?

Discussion:

- **(a)** She can make a rectangle of 140 square feet by using dimensions of 4' by 10" (perimeter of 48').
- **(b)** The maximum rectangle she can create having a perimeter of 48' would be a square of 12' on a side.

Teacher's Notes:

ACTIVITY 46   **Title:** "A Piece of Pi"

Purpose and Topic: This activity provides students with a means of determining the relationship between the circumference and the diameter of circular figures.

Materials: The top from a coffee can, a pie tin, a small can, or any other circular or cylindrical objects; a supply of masking tape; tape measures; Reproduction Page 33 and toothpicks (for Extension)

How to Use It: Divide the class into groups. Give each group two of the objects and some masking tape. Have each group put masking tape around the circular edge of each object with no overlap. Remove the tape and stretch it out onto the top of the desk. Now have students place the circular object on the tape and mark off the diameter as many times as possible. Each group should obtain a result that shows the circumference to be a little more than three times the diameter. Have each group share their results. The students have now "discovered" π (pi), which equals a little more than 3 (3.1416). Students may use a tape measure instead.

Extension: The number π has always fascinated mathematicians, and there have been many methods found for approximating π. This extension, discovered by Count Buffon in 1777, is a probability experiment that yields an approximate value for π. You will need a copy of Reproduction Page 33 and 10 pieces of a toothpick, each 1 cm in length.

Give each group of students a copy of Reproduction Page 33 and a supply of 10 toothpick pieces. From a reasonable height, have the students drop the toothpicks onto the grid. One student should now count the number of "hits"—that is, when a toothpick lands on, crosses, or touches one of the grid lines. Repeat this experiment a total of 10 times. Combine the results and form a fraction:

$$\frac{\text{Total number of toothpicks dropped (100)}}{\text{Total number of "hits"}}$$

Use a calculator and perform the division. The result should approximate π. Now, combine the data for the entire class and again perform the division. The result should be an even better approximation of π. (*Note:* You can use any ruled surface where the lines are d units apart and the length of the toothpick pieces is $d/2$.)

Problem 1:   Tennis balls are usually tightly packed in a cylindrical can containing three balls. Is the height of the can greater than, equal to, or less than the circumference? Explain.

Discussion: As shown in this figure, the height of the can is 3 diameters, or 3d. The circumference is πd, approximately 3.14d. Thus, the circumference is larger than the height.

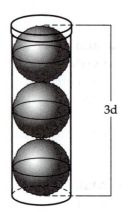

Problem 2:   A tin can of tuna fish has a diameter of 3". The company has just come out with a new, larger can. The label of this new can is 3" longer than the label on the original can. What is the diameter of the new can?

Discussion: The circumference of the original can is πd, which equals 3π, or approximately 9.42". The new can has a circumference of 12.42" (3" more than the original). The new diameter will be 12.42 ÷ π, or approximately 3.95".

Teacher's Notes:

ACTIVITY 47   **Title:**   "Area of a Circle"

Purpose and Topic: This aid, although informal and approximate, permits one to develop the formula for the area of a circle. Students must have previously learned the formulas for the circumference of a circle ($C = 2\pi r$) and the area of a parallelogram ($A = bh$)

Materials: A circle drawn on poster-board or a copy of Reproduction Page 34

How to Make It: Draw a circle on poster-board and divide it into 16 congruent sectors, as shown here (or use the circle shown on Reproduction Page 34):

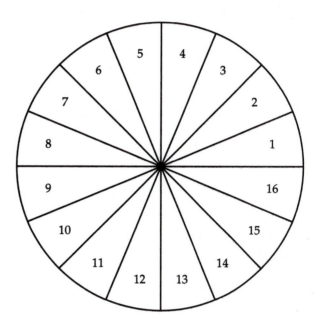

How to Use It: Have the students cut the 16 sectors apart. Place them in alternating positions, as shown here:

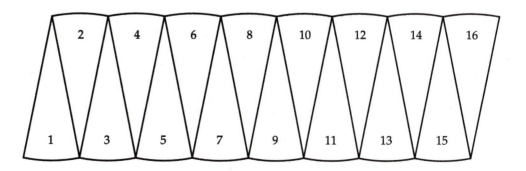

The figure now *approximates* a parallelogram. The difference is that the base is a series of arcs, rather than a straight line segment. The base of the parallelogram is therefore half the circumference, and the height equals the radius. The area of the parallelogram is given by the formula $A = bh$. Thus:

$A = b \times h$
$A = (1/2)(C)(r)$
$A = (1/2)(2\pi r)(r)$
$A = \pi r^2$

Extension: Divide the class into groups. Have each group take a circle and divide it into a different number of congruent sectors (e.g., 8, 24, 36, etc.). Have them cut the sectors apart and arrange them to form a parallelogram as previously done. Have them trace the perimeter of the resulting "parallelogram." Ask them for a conclusion. They should discover that the greater the number of sectors, the closer the figure becomes to a parallelogram.

Problem 1: A furniture company is making table tops by cutting circular cross-sections from a mahogany tree. To order the proper amount of polyurethane needed to finish the table tops, the company must know the approximate area of each cross section in advance. The circumference of the tree is about 11 feet. What is the approximate area of one table top?

Discussion: The circumference of the cross section is 11 feet.

$C = \pi d$
$11 = \pi d$
$11 = (22/7)d$
$3.5 = d$

The radius is 1.75 or 7/4.

$A = \pi r^2$
$A = (49/16)(22/7)$
$A = 77/8 = 9.6$

The area of a cross section is approximately 9.6 square feet.

Problem 2: An old-fashioned bicycle has a rear wheel with a 28" diameter and a front wheel with a 14" diameter. If the bicycle travels 1 mile, which wheel makes more rotations? How many more? (Use $\pi = 22/7$.)

Discussion:

5,280 feet = 1 mile
$5{,}280 \times 12 = C \times ($ the number of rotations$)$

Rear Wheel

$$\frac{5280 \times 12}{28 \times 22/7} = \frac{63360}{88} = 720 \text{ rotations}$$

Front Wheel

$$\frac{5280 \times 12}{14 \times 22/7} = \frac{63360}{44} = 1440 \text{ rotations}$$

$$1440 - 720 = 720$$

The front wheel makes 720 more rotations.

Some students will realize that circumference is a linear relationship with respect to the diameters. Therefore, they need only find the number of rotations for one wheel and either multiply or divide by 2 to find the other.

Teacher's Notes:

ACTIVITY 48   **Title:** "Polyominoes"

Purpose and Topic: Polyominoes can be used to explore congruence, area, perimeter, symmetry, and transformations.

Materials: Graph paper; Reproduction Page 35; scissors; a set of small 1" × 1" squares made from cardboard, poster-board, or oak-tag

How to Make It: For the last section of this activity, each student will be given a copy of Reproduction Page 35, which contains the set of 12 pentominoes. They will be asked to cut out the set. The same shapes can be copied onto oak-tag or light cardboard and then cut out. This will provide a more permanent set of pentominoes.

How to Use It: Begin the lesson by discussing polyominoes in general. A polyomino is simply two or more square regions with a side in common. Divide the class into small groups of four or five students. Distribute the 1" × 1" squares to each group, along with several sheets of the graph paper. Have them construct the set of *dominoes* (two squares) and the set of *trominoes* (three squares) and draw them on the graph paper. There is only one domino and only two trominoes, as shown here:

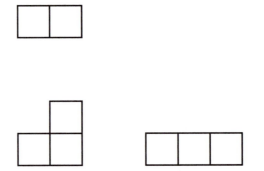

Students should understand that a flip or turn of a polyomino does not create a new shape; the "flipped" polyomino is still congruent to the original. Find and discuss the area and perimeter of each polyomino in the set.

Next, have the class consider the set of *tetrominoes* (four squares). Have them build as many of these as they can and sketch them on the graph paper. Have a representative from each group sketch one tetromino on the board until all five have been discovered (as shown here). Find and discuss the perimeter and area of each.

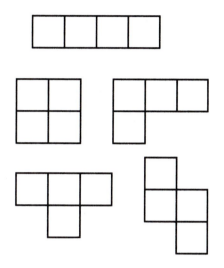

Now, have each group form as many *pentominoes* as possible (five square regions). After they have made a pentomino shape, have them sketch it on graph paper at their table. See how many the groups can find. After the class has discovered all they can (there are exactly 12, shown here) pass out a copy of Reproduction Page 35 to each student. Have the students cut out their own set of pentominoes. Find and discuss the perimeter and area of each pentomino.

Ask the groups to see if they can arrange one set of the 12 pentominoes into a rectangle. Some mathematicians claim that there are more than 200 ways to do this. Here is one such arrangement, namely a 6" × 10" rectangle:

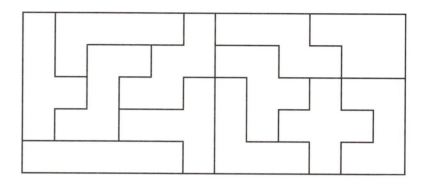

Notice that this can be split into two rectangles, each 5" × 6" and then rearranged to form a 5" × 12" rectangle, as follows. Discuss the perimeter and area of each figure.

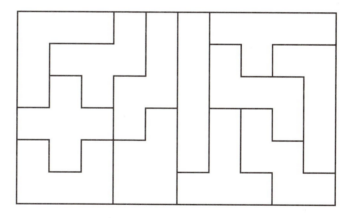

Extension: A rather obvious extension is to have the class find all the possible *hexominoes*, different arrangements of six squares. This is a rather lengthy project, since there are 35 different hexominoes. A class project might be to place a large sheet of graph paper on a bulletin board and have each new hexomino drawn on it as it is discovered.

Problem 1: Which of the 12 pentominoes shown earlier can be folded to make a "box" without a top? (There are 8 of them.)

Discussion: Students may wish to take their set of 12 pentominoes and actually fold them to see which form a box. The ones circled here can be folded in this manner:

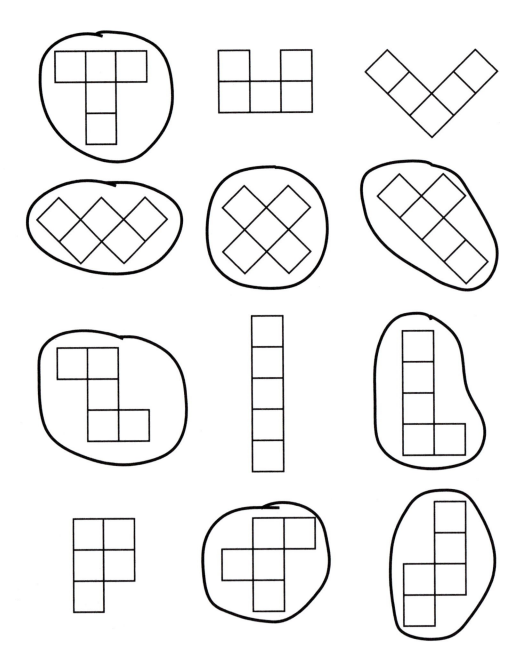

Problem 2: Assume that the side of each square used on your set of pentominoes is 1 unit. Find the perimeter and area of each of the 12 pentominoes. Which shape has the maximum perimeter? The minimum perimeter? The maximum area? The minimum area?

Discussion: Obviously, the area of each pentomino will be the same (namely, 5 square units), since each is made up of 5 congruent squares. However, the perimeters are not all the same. One pentomino has a perimeter of 10 units; the rest have a perimeter of 12 units.

Problem 3: There are 10 people waiting to be seated in a restaurant. The restaurant owner is placing square tables so that they touch. Each table can seat 1 person on a side. What is the number of tables needed to seat the 10 people, and how should they be arranged?

Discussion: Three square tables are needed, if they are grouped with vertex touching vertex. If adjacent sides are placed together, four tables are needed. They can be arranged in a variety of ways.

Teacher's Notes:

ACTIVITY 49   **Title:** "Models of the Regular Polyhedrons"

Purpose and Topic: One of the many skills teachers try to develop in geometry is the ability of pupils to visualize, discover, and express relationships when working with solid figures. Unfortunately, textbooks can show only two-dimensional pictures of three-dimensional figures. These models of the five regular polyhedrons (tetrahedron, hexahedron [cube], octahedron, dodecahedron, and icosahedron) are easy to construct. They are made up of plane figures, with which the students should already be familiar.

Materials: Reproduction Pages 36 through 40; scissors, tape

How to Make It: Give each student or group of students a copy of the five Reproduction Pages 36 through 40. Have the students cut the models out carefully along the solid lines. The models should then be carefully creased, folded along the dotted lines, and then taped into place. (*Note:* The models can be used "as is" or the dimensions can be enlarged.)

How to Use It: After the students have made their own set of polyhedrons, they should be asked to complete the following table:

Figure	Number of Faces (*F*)	Number of Vertices (*V*)	Number of Edges (*E*)
Tetrahedron	4	4	6
Hexahedron (cube)			
Octahedron			
Dodecahedron			
Icosahedron			

Once the table has been completed, ask the students to find a relationship between the number of faces (*F*), vertices (*V*), and edges (*E*). With help, they will be able to discover Euler's Law—namely, $F + V = E + 2$.

Extensions: An excellent show-type project is to make the models in different sizes and on different kinds of paper. Gift wrapping paper makes beautiful models. When these models have been completed, they can be strung with black thread and hung from wire clothes hangers to make a set of math mobiles to suspend around the classroom.

Another activity is to have the students in the class take their models and determine which, when put together, form a solid figure with no space between them.

Problem 1:   Number the eight vertices of a cube from 1 through 8 so that the sum of the numbers on each face is 18.

Discussion: By guess and test, students find that in order to get a sum of 18 by using 4 addends, 0, 2, or 4 of them must be odd numbers. You must use exactly two of them on each face, since 0 or 4 will not yield a sum of 18. Place 1 and 7 on the opposite vertices of the top face and place 3 and 5 on the opposite vertices of the bottom face. The face containing 1 and 7 must have 4 and 6, whereas 2 and 8 are placed with 3 and 5.

Top face:	1, 4, 7, 6 (clockwise)
Bottom face:	2, 3, 5, 8 (clockwise)

Problem 2: The students in the workshop have constructed a five-layer mobile out of unit cubes glued face to face. The first three layers are shown here:

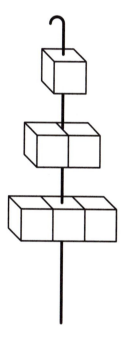

Medallions are then placed on each of the exposed faces to reflect the sun. How many medallions are needed for the entire mobile?

Discussion:

Row Number	Number of Medallions	Total Number
1	6	6
2	10	16
3	14	30
4	18	48
5	22	70

They will need 70 medallions.

For the more experienced students, you may wish to extend this to determine the formula for the number of medallions in each row and the total number of medallions for any number of rows. For each row, the number of medallions (faces) = $4n + 2$. For the total number, the formula is $2n(n + 2)$. Note that both yield only even answers.

Teacher's Notes:

ACTIVITY 50   **Title:** "Volume of a Box"

Purpose and Topic: Students will be introduced to volume and the use of graphs to show data.

Materials: Several sheets of paper or light cardboard, each 9" × 12"; scissors; tape; rulers

How to Make It: Divide the class into small groups. Provide each group with six sheets of the 9" × 12" paper, a ruler, a pair of scissors, and some tape. Ask each group to create a series of open "boxes" (without tops) by cutting out square corners with dimensions of 1" × 1", 2" × 2", 3" × 3", and 4" × 4". They then fold the sides and use the tape to form the box together, as follows:

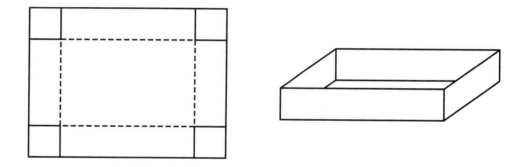

Now ask the students to estimate which of their boxes holds the most—that is, which has the greatest volume. After recording their guesses, actually compute the volume of each box by using the formula $v = lwh$.

Box	Side of Square Cut from Corner	$l \times w \times h$	Volume (V) (Cubic Inches)
#1	1"	$10 \times 7 \times 1$	70
#2	2"	$8 \times 5 \times 2$	80
#3	3"	$6 \times 3 \times 3$	54
#4	4"	$4 \times 1 \times 4$	16

If the students do not suggest it, ask if there might be another box with a volume larger than 80 cubic units. Have them make two new boxes by cutting out 1 1/2- and 2 1/2-inch squares. Notice that the length of the side of the square that is cut out is the height of the box. The box with a 1 1/2" height will have a volume of 81 cubic inches ($9 \times 6 \times 1 1/2$) ; the box with a 2 1/2" height will have a volume of 70 cubic inches ($7 \times 4 \times 2 1/2$). The students should recognize that the height of 1 1/2" yields the best estimate for a maximum volume. Now, have the students prepare a graph to show their data. They can use the horizontal axis as the height of the box in inches and use the vertical axis as the volume of the box in cubic inches. Find additional points by computation and connect the points with a smooth curve, as seen here:

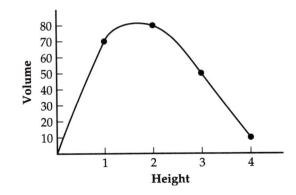

(The actual maximum volume is obtained when the side of the square is 1.7 inches.)

Problem 1:   The ABC Container Corporation has been given a contract to produce a container that will hold 16 1' × 1' × 1' cubes. What will be the dimensions of the container? Which will be the container with the least surface area?

Discussion: There are four possible containers, with surface areas as follows:

Dimensions	Surface Area
1 × 1 × 16	66 square feet
1 × 2 × 8	52 square feet
1 × 4 × 4	48 square feet
2 × 2 × 4	40 square feet

The 2' × 2' × 4' container has the least surface area.

Problem 2:   A rectangular box is being wrapped for shipping. The box measures 12" × 12" × 36". A strip of tape is placed around the box lengthwise, and another strip is placed around the middle of the box. How much tape is used?

Discussion: The tape around the larger dimension requires 2 lengths and 2 widths. The tape around the middle requires 4 widths. Thus, it takes 2 lengths and 6 widths, which is 2(36) + 6(12) = 144 inches of tape.

Teacher's Notes:

ACTIVITY 51   **Title:** "Battleship"

Purpose and Topic: This activity, based on a commercial game, enables students to become familiar with the graphing of points in the Cartesian plane.

Materials: Reproduction Page 41

How to Make It: Divide the class into pairs. Each student receives a copy of Reproduction Page 41, which shows the "Shot Grid" (to be used as a record of his or her "shots") and the "Battleship Grid" (to be used as a record of where his or her "battleships" have been placed as well as the opponent's "shots"). Each student draws three "battleships" anywhere on his or her Battleship Grid as follows: a 1 × 2 rectangle, a 1 × 3 rectangle, and a 1 × 4 rectangle. These must be placed either horizontally or vertically, but not diagonally. Students are not to reveal the location of their ships to their opponent.

How to Use It: After both players have drawn their battleships on their own Battleship Grids, play begins. Players decide who goes first, and then alternate turns. The first player calls out the coordinates of a square in which he or she thinks an opponent's "battleship" lies. At the same time, the player places a circle on his or her Shot Grid in the appropriate box. A "hit" is defined as a box on the grid in which part of a battleship lies. If a hit is made, the opponent must say "Hit." At this time, the player fills in the oval on his or her Shot Grid, indicating a hit. If there is no "hit," the player says, "Miss." In either case, play resumes with the opponent choosing a location. When all the squares in the grid that represents the player's ship have been filled in, the player must announce, "You have sunk my '2' ship," or "You have sunk my '3' ship," and so on. The game continues until one player's ships have all been "sunk." If time interrupts, the player with more "hits" is declared the winner. (*Note:* In this game, the coordinates identify a region on the grid. Students should be informed that, in graphing, an ordered pair represents a point, not a region. A sample pair of grid cards are shown here:

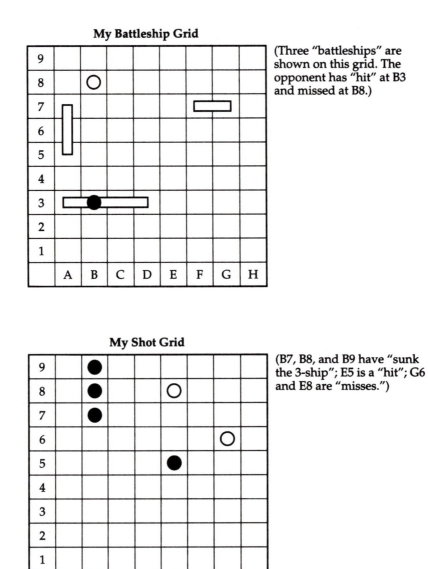

My Battleship Grid

(Three "battleships" are shown on this grid. The opponent has "hit" at B3 and missed at B8.)

My Shot Grid

(B7, B8, and B9 have "sunk the 3-ship"; E5 is a "hit"; G6 and E8 are "misses.")

Extension: This extension is called "Where Am I?" Students make a design by shading in four or five regions on the game board. The regions must touch at a point or a line (they cannot be scattered.) The game is played with the same rules as Battleship.

Problem 1: In an arcade game, John moves his tank from the home base as follows: 4 units due east, 6 units due north, 1 unit due east, and 6 units due north. From that point, he moved his tank back to the home base by the shortest possible route. How many units was his total trip?

Discussion: The figure results in a right triangle with a horizontal dimension of 5 units, a vertical dimension of 12 units, and the hypotenuse, therefore, of 13 units. John's total trip was 30 units.

Problem 2:   Using the following figure, how many paths exactly 4 units long are there to go from A to C?

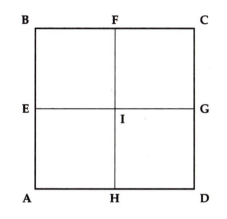

Discussion: There are six paths as listed:

A-B-C	A-E-I-F-C	A-E-I-G-C
A-D-C	A-H-I-F-C	A-H-I-G-C

Teacher's Notes:

CHAPTER FOUR

Algebra

ACTIVITY 52   **Title:** "It All Adds Up!"

Purpose and Topic: This activity provides students with practice in adding integers.

Materials: Reproduction Page 42

How to Use It: Give each student a copy of Reproduction Page 42. Using the circles already filled in, the students are to fill in the empty circles in the drawing. The number in each circle is the sum of the two circles immediately beneath it. The completed drawings are shown here:

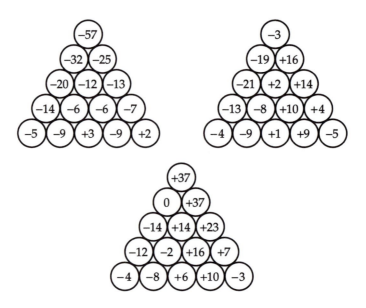

Extension: Have students create arrays of their own, similar to the ones shown. This is most easily done by filling in the bottom row of circles in the array, and then adding up to obtain the top circle. They then erase the numbers in those circles they feel are not necessary. They can then exchange papers with a neighbor and try to figure out each other's array. (*Note:* The final or top circle must be filled in to serve as a checkpoint for the entire array.)

Problem 1: The Fibonacci sequence 1, 1, 2, 3, 5, 8, 13, 21,...is a well-known sequence of numbers. Each term after the first two is found by adding the previous two terms. What would be the six terms immediately preceding the 1, 1, 2?

Discussion:

> The term preceding 1 must be 0, since $0 + 1 = 1$.
> The term preceding 0 must be 1, since $1 + 0 = 1$.
> The term preceding 1 must be -1, since $-1 + 1 = 0$.
> The term preceding -1 must be $+2$, since $2 + (-1) = 1$.
> The term preceding $+2$ must be -3, since $-3 + 2 = -1$.
> The term preceding -3 must be $+5$, since $5 + (-3) = 2$.
>
> The sequence would be 5, -3, 2, -1, 1, 0, 1, 1, 2, 3, 5, 8,...

Problem 2: The lowest surface temperature ever recorded in the United States was $-80°$ F, measured in Alaska. The highest temperature ever recorded was 214° F higher, recorded in Death Valley. What was the record high temperature?

Discussion: Students add $(-80) + (214) = 134°$ F.

Teacher's Notes:

ACTIVITY 53   **Title:** "Integer Racetrack"

Purpose and Topic: Students practice addition and subtraction of integers in a game setting. In addition, they develop a strategy for deciding on a given operation.

Materials: Integer Racetrack game board; a spinner (Reproduction Page 43; brass fastener; game pieces)

How to Make It: Prepare a game board for each pair of students, as shown here. The game board should show a number line going from +15 to –15.

In addition, cut out the spinner shown on Reproduction Page 43. Either paste this on a piece of oak-tag or copy it onto oak-tag. The remainder of the spinner can be made from a bent paper clip and a brass fastener.

How to Use It: Each student selects a game piece and places it on the game board at 0. One player's goal is +15; the other player's goal is –15. In turn, each player spins the spinner. The position to which the marker is moved is the result of either adding or subtracting the number on the spinner to or from the player's position on the number line. A player must move in turn; he or she cannot stand still. Players alternate turns until one player lands exactly on his or her target number. Players cannot go beyond +15 or –15. The winning player receives a score equal to the distance between the opponent's position and his or her goal. Players now place their markers back at 0 and change target directions. That is, the player who was moving toward +15 now moves toward –15 and vice versa. After the two rounds are completed, the player with the higher score is the winner.

Extension: One variation of the game is that only addition may be used (or only subtraction). A player who goes beyond his or her goal loses the game.

Problem 1: On the 2:00 weather broadcast, the current temperature was 18° F, but the wind chill temperature was –4° F. What was the difference between the wind chill temperature and the actual temperature?

Discussion: The difference is always the absolute value. Thus, the difference between 18° F and –4° F is 22°.

Problem 2: Dolores and Rosalie started out on their bikes from the town square. Dolores rode 8 miles east and then 2 miles west. Rosalie rode 4 miles west and then 10 miles east. How far apart were they?

Discussion: Use a number line with east as + and west as –:

Dolores: $(+8) + (-2) = +6$
Rosalie: $(-4) + (+10) = +6$

They are together, 0 miles apart.

Teacher's Notes:

ACTIVITY 54   **Title:** "What's My Rule?"

Purpose and Topic: This activity provides students with practice in mental arithmetic using their arithmetic operations.

Materials: None

How to Use It: The teacher selects one of the ten given rules. Ask one student to select any two integers. The teacher responds with the "answer," arrived at by applying the rule. Continue having different students select pairs of numbers to which responses are given according to the rule. When a student thinks that he or she has discovered the rule, do not ask for the rule. Instead, give the student two numbers and see if he or she gives the correct response. If so, ask him or her to reveal the rule. If not, continue asking for number pairs. Once a student has discovered the rule, that student becomes the leader of the next game. Supply the student with one of the rules given, or ask the student to develop his or her own rule.
   Here are the 10 rules:

(a) $a + b$ For example, if a student gives +5 and –7, the answer is –2.
(b) $a + b - 1$ For example, if a student gives 4 and 3, the answer is 6.
(c) $(a + b)/2$ For example, if a student gives 5 and 7, the answer is 6. If a student gives 5 and 8, the answer is 6 1/2.
(d) $ab - 3$ For example, if a student gives –5 and +8, the response is –43. If a student gives +1 and +2, the response is –1.
(e) $12 - (a + b)$ For example, if a student gives 3 and 4, the response is 5. If a student gives 9 and 5, the response is –2.
(f) $a + ab$ For example, if a student gives –2 and +5, the answer is –12.
(g) $a^2 + b^2$ For example, if a student gives +2 and –4, the answer is 20.
(h) $a^2 - b^2$ For example, if a student gives +3 and –4, the answer is –7.
(i) $2a - 3b$ For example, if a student gives 2 and –3, the answer is 13.
(j) a^2 For example, if a student gives –3, the answer is +9.

Extension: In the original activity, the students provided the "input" while the leader provided the "rule" and the "output." In this extension, the leader supplies the "rule" and the "output," while the students are asked to find an "input." There will usually be more than one possible input. For example, if the rule is $a^2 + b$ and the answer is 9, then there are 6 possible inputs:

$a = 1, \quad b = 8$	$a = 2, \quad b = 5$	$a = 3, \quad b = 0$
$a = -1, \quad b = 8$	$a = -2, \quad b = 5$	$a = -3, \quad b = 0$

This activity illustrates the idea of a function—multiple inputs that lead to a unique answer.

Problem: When a local TV station televises a hit program, it sells advertising time. A program costs the station $5,000, and there are 15 minutes of advertising time.

(a) Find the profit if the price per advertising minute is $450.

(b) How much must the advertising price per minute be to make a profit of $2,200, if there are only 12 advertising minutes?

(c) Write a formula for profit (*p*) in terms of the number of minutes (*m*), the cost per minute (*c*), and the cost for the program, (*D*).

Discussion:

(a) 15 minutes × $450 = $6,750
$6,750 − $5,000 = $1,750 profit

(b) $5,000 + $2,200 = $7,200
$7,200 ÷ 12 = $600 per advertising minute

(c) $p = m \times c - D$

Teacher's Notes:

ACTIVITY 55   **Title:** "Expression 21"

Purpose and Topic: This game provides students with practice in evaluating simple linear and quadratic expressions. At the same time, students must make decisions under a strategy game setting.

Materials: 9 cards of one color or size; 36 cards of a different color or size

How to Make It: The deck is made up of two parts: 9 "Value Cards" and 36 "Expression Cards." To make the Value Cards, write the number 1, 2, or 3 on each of three cards (total: 9 cards). Make the Expression Cards by writing one of the following algebraic expressions on each of three cards (total: 36 cards):

$$x, \qquad x^2, \qquad x + 1, \qquad x^2 + 1, \qquad x - 1, \qquad x^2 - 1, \qquad x + 2,$$
$$x^2 + x, \qquad x^2 - x, \qquad x - 2, \qquad x + 3, \qquad x + 4$$

How to Use It: This is a game for two, three, or four players. Begin by deciding which player will be the dealer. The dealer shuffles the nine Value Cards and places them face down in the center of the playing area. The dealer then deals two Expression Cards, one face up and one face down, to each player, including himself or herself. The dealer turns the top Value Card face up. Each player now evaluates his or her two expressions using the value shown on the Value Card. The sum of the two Playing Cards is calculated. Each player in turn must now decide whether to continue. If a player continues, the dealer deals him or her another card and the player recalculates his or her sum. The object of the game is to get a sum as close to 21 as possible without going over. Players do not need to reveal their hidden cards unless they have gone over 21. The dealer goes last, after each player has decided to stop or has gone over 21. Each player (who has not gone over 21) receives 1 point if he or she is closer to 21 than the dealer. Every player the dealer beats (including those who have gone over 21) gives the dealer 1 point. If a player and the dealer have the same sum, no points are given. The winner is the first player to reach 15 points. After each round, the deal rotates.

Problem: In 1998, the cost of first-class mail was given by the equation:

$$C = .32 + .23\,(n - 1)$$

where C = the total cost in dollars and n = the number of ounces.

(a) How much would it cost to mail a first-class letter that weighed 3 ounces?
(b) How much would it cost to mail a first-class letter that weighed 4.3 ounces?
(c) What is the weight of a first-class letter that costs $1.01 to mail?

Discussion:

(a) $C = .32 + .23 (n - 1)$
$C = .32 + .23 (3 - 1)$
$C = .32 + .46$
$C = .78$ or 78¢

(b) This problem requires some knowledge of postage rates. Cost is only calculated using whole number weights, which are rounded up! Thus, 4.3 ounces becomes 5 ounces.
$C = .32 + .23 (n - 1)$
$C = .32 + 4 (.23)$
$C = 1.24$ or $1.24

(c) A table will help:
Greater than 0 ounces, up to and including 1 ounce = .32
Greater than 1 ounce, up to and including 2 ounces = .55
Greater than 2 ounces, up to and including 3 ounces = .78
Greater than 3 ounces, up to and including 4 ounces = 1.01

The weight is greater than 3 ounces but less than or equal to 4 ounces.

Teacher's Notes:

ACTIVITY 56 **Title:** "Find the Value"

Purpose and Topic: This game provides students with the opportunity to evaluate algebraic expressions with integers.

Materials: 24 Expression Cards of one color or size; 7 Value Cards of another color or size

How to Make It: To make the 7 Value Cards, write one of the integers from -3 to $+3$ on each card. To make the Expression Cards, write one of the following expressions on each card:

$x + 1$	$2(x + 2)$	$x/2$	$(x/2) - 1$	$2x + 3$
$3x - 4$	$x^2 - 2$	$2x^2$		
$y - 1$	$2(y - 2)$	$(3y - 2)/3$	$3y/2$	$3y + 1$
$1 - 3y$	y^2	$y^2 - 1$		
$z + 3$	$3 - z$	$2(z + 1)$	$(z/2) - 2$	$5z + 1$
$2 - z^2$	$2 + z^2$	$4/(z - 4)$		

How to Use It: This is a game for four players. Begin by deciding who will be the dealer. The dealer shuffles the Expression Cards and deals six to each player, including herself or himself. The dealer now shuffles the Value Cards, places them face down on the table, and turns up the top Value Card. He or she leads by placing one of his or her Expression Cards face up on the table. Using the number on the upturned Value Card and evaluating his or her Expression Card, the dealer calls out his or her result. The other players in turn must play an Expression Card with the same variable and call out their values. The player with the Expression Card of highest value takes the trick. A trick consists of 5 cards—the 4 Expression Cards and the 1 Value Card. (*Note:* If a player cannot play an Expression Card with the same variable as the dealer, he or she plays any Expression Card from his or her hand and passes; the player cannot win that trick. After each trick, a new Value Card is turned face up and the lead rotates.)

In case of a tie for the highest value, the cards in that trick are awarded to the player who wins the next round. The game ends after six rounds. Each player receives one point for each Expression Card, plus the sum of the integers on his or her Value Cards. The player with the highest score is the winner.

Extension: An extension to this game would be to change the method of scoring as follows. A player's final score is calculated by adding the numbers on the Value Cards plus the value of all his or her Expression Cards using the one remaining (the seventh) Value Card.

Problem 1:   A flock of Canadian geese flew 800 miles in d days across the country to reach their winter home. Write an expression to represent the average number of miles the flock flew each day. Find the average number of miles they flew each day if the trip took 4 days.

Discussion: The formula is $800/d$ = the average number of miles per day. Thus, for 4 days, the flock flew $800/4 = 200$ miles per day.

Problem 2:   Amanda must earn 300 points to win a giant stuffed panda. She already has 189 points. Which of the following could be used to find p, the number of points Amanda must still earn?

(a) $189 + p = 300$ **(c)** $189 + 300 = p$
(b) $189 - p = 300$ **(d)** $189 \div p = 300$

Discussion: The correct answer is (a). Multiple-choice questions are commonly asked of students on tests.

Teacher's Notes:

ACTIVITY 57   **Title:** "I'll Guess Your Number!"

Purpose and Topic: This is a number game that the teacher plays with a group of students. It involves mental computations, and, for those students with an algebra background, it provides the chance to discover "why it works."

Materials: None

How to Use It: Choose one student to perform the computation. Here are the directions the teacher gives to the student. (The algebraic "proof" will be shown alongside.)

Directions	Proof
(a) Select any two numbers from 1 to 9 and show them to the other students. (The teacher turns his or her head so that the numbers cannot be seen.)	x, y
(b) Select one of the two numbers and double it.	$2x$
(c) Add 18 to your product.	$2x + 18$
(d) Multiply the sum by 5.	$(2x + 18)5 = 10x + 90$
(e) Add your second number to this product.	$10x + 90 + y$
(f) Subtract 90 from the new sum.	$10x + 90 + y - 90 = 10x + y$
(g) Your original numbers were x and y.	

Here is an example:

Step (a)   The student chooses 6 and 8.
Step (b) $2 \times 6 = 12$
Step (c) $12 + 18 = 30$
Step (d) $30 \times 5 = 150$
Step (e) $150 + 8 = 158$
Step (f) $158 - 90 = 68$
Step (g)   The numbers are 6 and 8.

Extension: There are many number "tricks" available; here is another one you might wish to try. Ask someone in the class to pick a number. Tell the person that when the game is over, the answer will be 8. The individual is not to tell you his or her number.

Step (a)	Select any number.	x
Step (b)	Add 6.	$x + 6$
Step (c)	Multiply by 4.	$(x + 6)4 = 4x + 24$
Step (d)	Add 8.	$4x + 24 + 8 = 4x + 32$
Step (e)	Divide by 4.	$4x + 32 \div 4 = x + 8$
Step (f)	Subtract your original number.	$x + 8 - x = 8$
Step (g)	Your answer is 8.	

Problem: The formula $r \times t = d$ gives distance traveled in terms of rate and time. Write an expression that can be used to find the time it takes to travel a given distance. Use your formula to find the time it takes to travel 800 miles at a speed of 40 miles per hour.

Discussion:

$r \times t = d$
$t = d/r$
$t = 800/4 = 20$ hours

Teacher's Notes:

ACTIVITY 58   **Title:**   "Algebra Tic-Tac-Toe"

Purpose and Topic: This activity provides practice in solving linear equations and evaluating algebraic expressions in a game setting.

Materials: Reproduction Page 44; a set of twenty-five 3" × 5" cards

How to Make It: On each of the 25 3" × 5" cards, write one of the following expressions, together with the number of that expression (answers are given in parentheses):

1. The largest prime number less than 20.   (19)
2. The first prime number greater than 20.   (23)
3. The number whose prime factorization is $3^2 \cdot 2$.   (18)
4. If $3x + 5 = 65$, then $x = ?$ (20)
5. If $\sqrt{N} = 5$, then $N = ?$ (25)
6. The value of the expression $x + 7$ when $x = 4$ is?   (11)
7. If $6x = 4x + 28$, then $x = ?$ (14)
8. If $2x + 3x = 5$, then $x = ?$ (1)
9. The value of the expression $\dfrac{(-6)(8)}{(2)(-3)}$ is?   (8)
10. If $N^2 = 9$, then $N = ?$ (3)
11. The only even prime number is?   (2)
12. If $3x = 51$, then $x = ?$ (17)
13. $(+7) + (-3) =$ (4)
14. If $\sqrt{x} = 4$, then $x = ?$ (16)
15. A rectangle has an area of 200 square inches, a length
    of 20 inches, and a width of x inches. Then $x = ?$ (10)
16. If $10x - 6x = 28$, then $x = ?$ (7)
17. If $3x = 18$, then $x = ?$ (6)
18. The smallest number divisible by 3 and 5 is?   (15)
19. The square of 3 is?   (9)
20. If $5x + 3x = 40$, then $x = ?$ (5)
21. The value of the expression $x + 2x + 3x$ when $x = 4$ is?   (24)
22. The length of a side of a square whose area is
    169 square inches is?   (13)
23. If $2x + 5x = 84$, then $x = ?$ (12)
24. If $3x - 8 = 2x + 14$, then $x = ?$ (22)
25. If $2x = 42$, then $x = ?$ (21)

How to Use It: Give each student a copy of Reproduction Page 44. On the page are two 3 × 3 cell Tic-Tac-Toe boards. Have the students select any nine numbers from 1 through 25 and place them anywhere on the first card. Do the same with the second card. (*Note:* Students may select some of the same numbers to appear on both cards.)

Shuffle the deck of 25 cards and place it face down. Either the teacher or a student can serve as the "caller." The caller turns over the top card from the pack and reads the problem. Each student works out the answer.

If a student has this number on either of his or her cards, the student circles it and places the number of the expression in that cell. Play continues until one student has three circled answers in a row, horizontally, vertically, or diagonally. The caller checks the answers to be certain that they are correct and that they correspond to the appropriate expression number. The student who first gets Tic-Tac-Toe is the winner.

Extensions: The game can be made longer by requiring that all nine numbers be circled, or that only a horizontal or vertical row will win. You can also create other varieties of this game by replacing the 25 game cards with simple word problems or more difficult expressions/equations.

Problem 1: Phil buys and sells used comic books. He buys them at 6 for $3.00 and then sells them at 4 for $3.00. Yesterday, he made a $6.00 profit. How many comic books did he sell?

Discussion: Using unit pricing, you will get the following:

Comics cost: $3.00 ÷ 6 = 50¢ each
Comics sell: $3.00 ÷ 4 = 75¢ each

for a profit of 25¢ per comic book sold. To make a profit of $6.00, you take

$6.00 ÷ 25 = 24

Phil sold 24 comic books.
The problem can also be solved algebraically. Let x = the number of comic books sold:

$$\frac{3x}{4} - \frac{3x}{6} = 6$$
$$9x - 6x = 72$$
$$3x = 72$$
$$x = 24$$

Phil sold 24 comic books.

Problem 2: Jesse was doing his algebra homework. In the last problem, he was supposed to subtract a number from 150, but he made a mistake and added it to 150 instead. Jesse was even more surprised when his answer was exactly twice as much as it should have been. What was the number Jesse added?

Discussion: Let x = the number Jesse added:

$$2(150 - x) = 150 + x$$
$$300 - 2x = 150 + x$$
$$150 = 3x$$
$$50 = x$$

Jesse added 50.

Teacher's Notes:

ACTIVITY 59   **Title:** "Algebra Concentration"

Purpose and Topic: This activity provides practice for students in solving linear equations within a game setting.

Materials: One deck of 24 3" × 5" cards

How to Make It: On each of 12 cards, write one of the following equations:

$3x = x + 16$	$y + 3 = 5$	$z - 3 = 20$
$x + 7 = 3$	$3y - 4 = y + 18$	$z + 5 = 3$
$2x - 6 = 24$	$y + 4 = 4$	$z + 12 = 3$
$2x + 3 = 9$	$y - 7 = 0$	$2z - 6 = 6$

On each of the other 12 cards place one of the answers:

8	2	23
-4	11	-2
15	0	-9
3	7	6

How to Use It: This is a game for two, three, or four players. Begin by shuffling the 24 cards. Deal the cards, one at a time, face down, placing them into a 6 × 4 card array. The first player turns over any 2 cards from the array. If the cards turned match (i.e., one is the answer to the equation shown on the other), the player removes the 2 cards from the array and places them in his or her "pack." He or she then takes another turn by selecting another pair of cards, looking for a match. If the cards turned up do not match, they are turned face down in their original position. The next player attempts to find a pair that match by turning over 2 cards, one at a time. Play continues until all 12 matches have been found and all 24 cards have been removed from the array. The winner is the student with the most cards in his or her pack.

Extensions: The game can be made a bit easier by placing the 12 answer cards into one 4 × 3 card array and the 12 equation cards into another 4 × 3 array. Students then pick one card from each array when attempting to find a matching pair.

     The game can also be changed to include addition, subtraction, multiplication, and/or division of signed numbers, as well as more complicated equations.

     The number of cards can be increased to 36, resulting in a larger 6 × 6 card array. The larger the array, the more difficult it will be for students to find a match, especially at first.

Problem 1:   Liz wants to buy a new tape deck that costs $140. She has saved $63 from her job at the pizza shop. She decides she can save $11 each month. How long will it take Liz to buy the tape deck?

Discussion: Let m = the number of months it will take:

$$63 + 11m = 140$$
$$11m = 77$$
$$m = 7$$

It will take Liz 7 months to save the money to buy the tape deck.

Problem 2:   Martha has only dimes and quarters in her purse. She has 11 coins in all and they have a total value of $1.70. How many of each coin does she have?

Discussion: Let x = the number of quarters:

$$(11 - x) = \text{the number of dimes}$$
$$.25x + .10 (11 - x) = 1.70$$
$$25x + 10(11 - x) = 170$$
$$25x + 110 - 10x = 170$$
$$15x = 60$$
$$x = 4$$

Martha has 4 quarters and 7 dimes.

Teacher's Notes:

ACTIVITY 60   **Title:**   "The Peg Game"

Purpose and Topic: This game provides students with the opportunity to recognize a pattern of moves. At the same time, it provides the data needed to develop an algebraic rule for that pattern.

Materials: Chips in each of two colors; Reproduction Page 45

How to Make It: Give each student a copy of Reproduction Page 45 and 10 chips—5 in each of two colors.

How to Use It: This is a game for an individual player. The player begins by placing the chips in the starting position, as follows:

The object of the game is to interchange the positions of the 10 chips in as few moves as possible. The students should keep track of the number of moves they make. Moves are made according to the following rules:

(a) Move only one chip at a time.
(b) A chip can be moved forward into an adjacent empty square.
(c) A chip can jump over a single chip of the other color into the next adjacent square if it is vacant. A chip may not jump over one of its own color.
(d) Chips can only move forward. (Moving backward would be undoing a previous move and thus the results would not be a "minimum" number of moves.)

After permitting the students to struggle with the game for a while, you might suggest that they use the *reduction and expansion* strategy of problem solving. Thus, they reduce the complexity of the game to one chip of each color and three boxes. They then move to two chips of each color and five boxes, and so on. They must keep track of their moves to help them look for a pattern as they proceed.

The following table shows the patterns of moves (using R to represent red chips and G to represent green chips).

Number of Chips of Each Color	Sequence of Moves	Number of Moves
1	RGR	3
2	RGGRRGGR	8
3	RGGRRRGGGRRRGGR	15
4	RGGRRRGGGGRRRRGGGRRRGGR	24
5	?	?

You may have to help the students find the rule governing the number of moves necessary. To do this, ask them to notice that one chip of each color requires 3, or (1 × 3), moves; two of each color requires 8, or (2 × 4), moves; three of each color requires 15, or (3 × 5), moves; and so on. The algebraic rule you are seeking in terms of M, the number of moves, and n, the number of pairs of chips, is $M = n(n + 2)$. Thus, for the 5 chips of each color, you would require $5(5 + 2) = 5 \cdot 7 = 35$ moves. (*Note:* A more permanent version of the game can be made by replacing the chips with golf tees and the game board with a strip of wood with 11 holes, equally spaced, in a single row.)

Have the students describe the pattern of moves for five chips of each color, using the same RG notation as above. Discuss the pattern they see:

RGGRRRGGGGRRRRRGGGGGRRRRRGGGGGRRRRRGGGGGRRRGGR

The pattern, then, is 1 Red, 2 Green, 3 Red, 4 Green, 5 Red, 5 Green, 5 Red, 4 Green, 3 Red, 2 Green, 1 Red.

This algebraic rule, $M = n(n + 2)$, enables you to determine the number of moves for any number of chips.

Problem 1: During a rain delay at the baseball game, the ground crew covered the infield with a square plastic tarpaulin that was 8100 square feet in area. How large is each side of the tarpaulin?

Discussion:

$$x = \text{a side of the tarpaulin}$$
$$x \cdot x = 8100$$
$$x^2 = 8100$$
$$x = 90$$

The tarpaulin is 90 feet on each side.

Problem 2:   Len is designing a logo for the school baseball field. The pattern he has chosen is in the form of an isosceles triangle whose dimensions are 5, 5, and 9 inches. If the actual logo will have the longest side of 36 feet, how long must each of the other legs of the triangle be?

Discussion: Let x = the length of one leg of the triangle:

$$\frac{5}{x} = \frac{9}{36}$$
$$9x = 180$$
$$x = 20$$

The leg of the triangle will be 20 feet long.

Teacher's Notes:

ACTIVITY 61   **Title:**   "Tower of Hanoi"

Purpose and Topic: A valuable experience for students is to examine data and try to find a formula to describe it. This activity generates such data as well as the appropriate formula.

Materials: For each game, three sticks; a board; seven washers or discs of increasing size

How to Make It: Place the three sticks upright into the board as shown here:

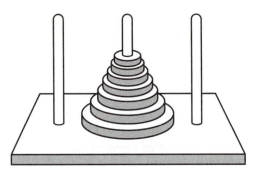

Put the seven discs in ascending size order on one of the poles as shown. (*Note:* A board with pegs is not necessary for the game. Students can use a piece of paper on which three squares are drawn. The discs are stacked in one square and must be moved to another.)

How to Use It: This is a game for an individual student or group of students working together. The object of the game is to move the entire pile of discs from one stick to a second one with a minimum number of moves. The final order of the discs must be the same as the original. The moves are made in accordance with two rules:

  (a) A larger disc can never be placed on top of a smaller disc.
  (b) Only one disc at a time can be moved.

(The third stick can be used as a "holding place" for some of the discs as they are moved.)
     Allow the students time to experiment with the game. Then suggest using *reduction and expansion,* as in Activity 60. Play the game first with one disc, then with two discs, then with three, and so on, keeping track of the moves. One disc obviously requires only one move. Two discs will require three moves. When three discs are used, it requires seven moves to complete the transfer. Keep track of the number of moves with a table:

Number of Discs	Minimum Number of Moves
1	1
2	3
3	7
4	15
5	31
6	?
7	?
.	.
.	.
.	.
n	M

The students should be familiar with the powers of 2 (2, 4, 8, 16, 32). They should recognize that each entry in the "Minimum Number of Moves" column is 1 less than a corresponding power of 2. Use this knowledge to help them develop the formula relating the number of discs (n) and the number of moves (M). The formula, $M = 2^n - 1$, will provide the answer to the number of moves needed for six discs (63) and for seven discs (127).

Extensions: An interesting Hindu tale says that Brahma placed 64 gold discs in the temple of Benares and called it the Tower of Brahma. The priests in the temple worked at moving the 64 discs in accordance with the two rules given earlier. The legend states that the world will come to an end when the movement is completed and all 64 discs have been transferred. Assuming that the priests can move 1 disc per second, have the students estimate how long it would take to move all 64 discs. Applying the formula, you obtain $2^{64} - 1 = 18{,}446{,}744{,}073{,}709{,}551{,}615$ seconds.

Problem: On June 1, Amy told a secret to her two friends, Abigail and Audrey. On June 2, Abigail told the secret to two friends, Betty and Barbara, and Audrey told the secret to two friends, Brenda and Bernice. On June 3, each of these four girls told the secret to two of their friends. This pattern continued until June 10th.

  (a) On June 10th, how many friends were told the secret?
  (b) On June 10th, how many people knew the secret?
  (c) Write a formula for the number of people who were told the secret on any given day.

Discussion: The number of people told the secret forms a pattern:

Day	Number Told	Total Who Know
1	2	3
2	4	7
3	8	15
4	16	31
.	.	.
.	.	.
.	.	.
10	1024	2047
.	.	.
.	.	.
.	.	.
n	2^n	$2^{n+1} - 1$

There were 1024 friends told on June 10th, and a total of 20,476 who knew the secret on June 10th.

Teacher's Notes:

ACTIVITY 62   **Title:**   "Model for $(a + b)^2 = a^2 + 2ab + b^2$"

Purpose and Topic: In a beginning algebra class, students often have trouble recognizing that the square of a binomial expression yields a trinomial expression. Most feel that there is a transitivity of an exponent over a sum. Thus, they think that $(a + b)^2 = a^2 + b^2$, forgetting the middle term, $2ab$. This device illustrates geometrically that there is a third term.

Materials: Poster-board or cardboard in various colors

How to Make It: Starting with a large piece of poster-board, cut it into a square, 10" on a side. Divide the square by marks, 3" from each vertex, as shown here:

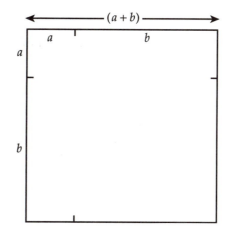

From a second piece of poster-board of a different color, cut a square piece, 3" (a) on a side. From a third piece, cut another square, 7" (b) on a side. From a fourth piece of poster-board, cut two rectangles, each 3" by 7" ($a \times b$).

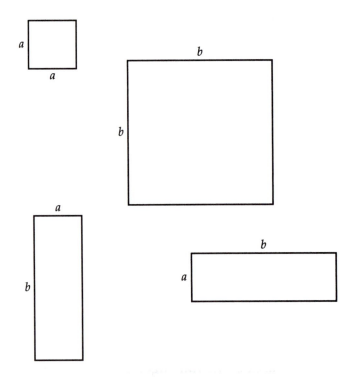

These four figures are then hinged into the appropriate positions on the base square with tape, and folded back until needed.

How to Use It: The original model is shown to the class, and a discussion of the meaning of $(a + b)^2$ should follow. This enables the students to visualize $(a + b)^2$ as the area of a square with side $(a + b)$. The pieces that have been hinged into place are now moved forward, one at a time. Thus, the square of side a has an area of a^2; the square of side b has an area of b^2. Students should notice at this point that there are two areas of the square still uncovered. These spaces are then covered by the two rectangles each having an area of $a \times b$. The completed model will then look like the following:

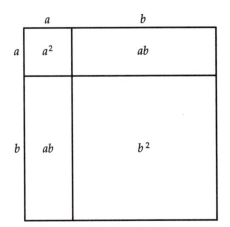

Problem 1: Jones Middle School is selling pages of advertising in the school yearbook. Each page is a square, and is divided into 4 sections, two rectangles and two squares, as shown here:

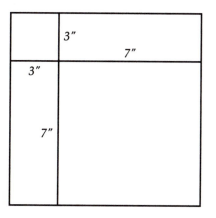

If the school charges $8 per square inch, what is the cost of a full page?

Discussion: There are several ways to solve this problem (i.e., to find the area of the full page). Some students may see that the page is 10" × 10" or 100 square inches $(a + b)^2$. Others may find the area of each of the four sections $(a^2 + b^2 + ab + ab)$. In either case, the page would cost $800.

Problem 2: Continue this sequence for 10 terms:

16, 49, 169, 256, . . .

Discussion: This sequence of terms is governed by the pattern rule $(a + b + c + \ldots)^2$, where a, b, and c are the individual digits. The sequence cycles rather quickly, since the next two terms are $(2 + 5 + 6)^2 = 169$, and $(1 + 6 + 9)^2 = 256$.

Problem 3: Continue this sequence for 10 terms:

16, 37, 58, 89, . . .

Discussion: Many students will suggest that the 89 is incorrect, and should be 79 (reflecting a constant difference of 21). However, the pattern rule for this sequence is $a^2 + b^2 + c^2 + \ldots$, where a, b, c, . . . are the individual digits. Thus, the completed sequence for 10 terms will be:

16, 37, 58, 89, 145, 42, 20, 4, 16, 37

Notice that the sequence has begun to cycle. This leads to an interesting mathematical fact: All numbers subjected to this pattern rule will cycle into a finite number of sequences. For example:

Start with 3: 3, 9, 81, 10, 1, 1, 1, 1, . . .
Start with 7: 7, 49, 97, 130, 10, 1, 1, 1, . . .
Start with 12: 12, 5, 25, 29, 85, 89, 145, 42, 20, 4, 16, 37, 58, 89, 145, . . .
Start with 2: 2, 4, 16, 37, 58, 89, 145, 42, 20, 4, 16, 37, . . .

Have students select other numbers to see what additional cycles they can discover.

Teacher's Notes:

ACTIVITY 63   **Title:**   "Model for $a^2 - b^2 = (a - b)(a + b)$"

Purpose and Topic: This physical model enables students to examine the relationship $a^2 - b^2 = (a - b)(a + b)$.

Materials: A square sheet of paper; scissors; ruler

How to Make It: Each student starts with a square sheet of paper, ABCD, as shown. This square has a side $= a$, and an area a^2.

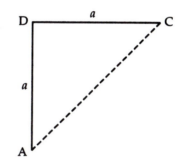

Fold the paper along the diagonal AC.

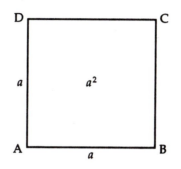

Next, fold point A a short distance (b) onto AD, and cut along the crease, EF, to remove the square with length b and area b^2.

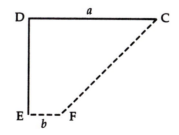

Now, unfold the sheet of paper. The figure has an area of $a^2 - b^2$.

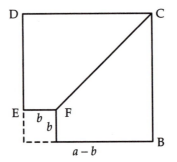

Cut along fold FC and rearrange the two figures to form a rectangle with sides $(a + b)$ and $(a - b)$.

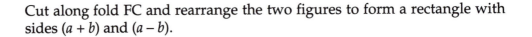

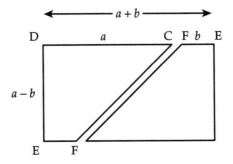

Thus, the area of the large figure must equal $a^2 - b^2$, since b^2 was removed several steps earlier. Yet it also equals $(a - b)(a + b)$. Hence $a^2 - b^2 = (a - b)(a + b)$.

Problem 1: Lorenzo has a square piece of wood that is 12" on a side that he wishes to use to form the front of a birdhouse. He cuts a 5" square window, 2 inches from the top, and 3 1/2 inches from either side, as shown in the diagram. What is the area of the remaining front of the birdhouse?

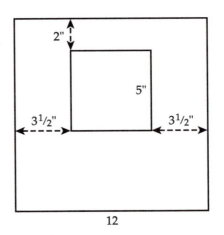

Solution: Students will probably draw a series of vertical and horizontal lines in an attempt to divide the figure into a series of rectangles, and then find the area of each. However, the students who have an insight into the situation, should realize that the area of the figure that remains is simply $a^2 - b^2$, or $12^2 - 5^2 = 144 - 25 = 119$ square inches. Since $a^2 - b^2 = (a + b)(a - b)$, the area you seek can also be found by $(12 + 5)(12 - 5) = (17)(7) = 119$.

Problem 2:   Suzanne has a plot of ground that is in the form of a square that is 17 feet on each side. She intends to make a rose garden within the plot that is in the shape of a square, 13 feet on each side. She will then tile the area between the two squares. What is the area that she plans to tile?

Discussion: A drawing will reveal that the answer is simply the difference between the areas of two squares—that is, $17^2 - 13^2$. Some students will then calculate the value of each term and find the difference: $289 - 169 = 120$ square feet. However, others may see that $17^2 - 13^2$ can be rewritten as $(17 - 13)(17 + 13) = (4)(30) = 120$ square feet.

An extension of this problem could be to ask the students to find the cost of tiling the border, if tiles come in squares 2' × 2' and cost $2.00 each. Insist that they explain their answer. (The answer is 30 tiles @ $2 each = $60). Notice that the placement of the interior square is virtually irrelevant, since tiles can be cut if necessary.

Teacher's Notes:

CHAPTER FIVE

Statistics and Probability

ACTIVITY 64   **Title:**   "What Does the Mean Really Mean?"

Purpose and Topic: This activity will help students understand the concept of the arithmetic mean. When most students are asked to explain what the arithmetic mean represents, they will usually explain how they obtained it. Most people interchange the terms *average* and *arithmetic mean*.

Materials: Chips or cubes; graph paper; Reproduction Page 46 (for Problem 1)

How to Make It: Divide the class into groups of four students. Give each group a bag of chips or cubes to use as manipulatives.

How to Use It: Follow these steps:

(a) Present the class with the following problem:

Four children brought cookies to school to share for snack time. Ariel brought 5 cookies, Bruce brought 10 cookies, Carrie brought 10 cookies, and Denise brought 7 cookies. They agreed that each person should have the same number of cookies. How could they do this? How many will each person have?

Have at least two groups explain how they solved the problem, and the answers they obtained.

(b) Add the following condition to the problem:

Ariel's friend, Eric, joined the group. He brought 6 cookies with him. Now how many cookies should each person get if they all have the same number? Are there any cookies left over? What should we do with these cookies?

Again, have at least two groups explain their solutions and their answers.

(c) Go back to the original problem. Lead the students to find a relationship between the number of cookies (5, 10, 10, 7), the total number of cookies (32), the number of students (4), and the number each child received (8). They should see that the arithmetic mean is the number that each person in a group would receive if they were to share the total number equally.

(d) Discuss the numbers above and below the average:

$$5 = 3 \text{ below} \quad (-3)$$
$$10 = 2 \text{ above} \quad (+2)$$
$$10 = 2 \text{ above} \quad (+2)$$
$$7 = 1 \text{ below} \quad (-1)$$

Notice how the numbers *above* and the numbers *below* add up to 0.

(e) Discuss the algorithm for computing the arithmetic mean of a set of numbers. Provide several examples for the students.

(f) Suppose another person joins the group and brings 15 cookies. Will the mean now go up, go down, or remain the same? Why?

Extensions: Here are three problems that should be discussed with the class:

(a) A group of four children has 48 cookies. How many does each person have? Ask several groups for their answers. (Does any group suggest 12-12-12-12?) Can they really tell how many each person has?

(b) The arithmetic mean of cookies for a group is 7. How many cookies does the group have altogether? (The answer cannot be determined unless the number of students in the group is known.) How many does each person have?

(c) A group of four students has 55 cookies. Could each person have the same number? Why?

Problem 1: Distribute a copy of Reproduction Page 46 to each student or group of students. Have them fill in the blank circles A, B, and C so that the middle number on each side is the arithmetic mean of the five numbers on that side.

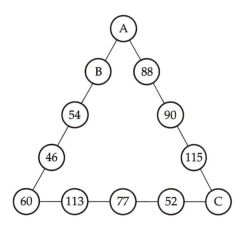

Discussion: Begin with the base of the triangle: Use the formula (algorithm) for the arithmetic mean:

$$\frac{60 + 113 + 77 + 52 + C}{5} = 77$$
$$302 + C = 385$$
$$C = 83$$

Next, take the right side of the triangle:

$$\frac{A + 88 + 90 + 115 + 83}{5} = 90$$
$$A + 376 = 450$$
$$A = 74$$

Finally,

$$\frac{74 + B + 54 + 46 + 60}{5} = 54$$
$$B + 234 = 270$$
$$B = 36$$

Problem 2: On six tests in which the scores can range from 0 to 100, Ira had an average of 90. What is the smallest score he could have had on any test?

Discussion: If the average (mean) for six tests is 90, then his total score must have been 6×90, or 540. In order to have a minimum score on any one test, the other five must be a maximum, or 100 each. For five tests, the maximum score would be 500. Therefore, the minimum score Ira could have had was 40.

Teacher's Notes:

ACTIVITY 65   **Title:**   "How Far Will It Roll?"

Purpose and Topic: Students will collect data in an experiment designed to determine the angle that causes a marble to roll the greatest distance.

Materials: 12" ruler; tubes from paper towels; marbles; protractors; tape measure; tape; Reproduction Page 47

How to Make It: Give each group of students a tube, a marble, a protractor, a tape measure, tape, and a copy of Reproduction Page 47. Have them fasten the 12" ruler to a vertical wall, as shown here:

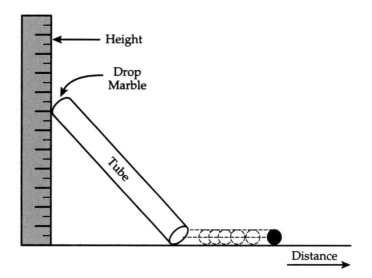

How to Use It: Divide the class into groups of four or five students. Each group of students tapes the top of the tube to a point along the vertical ruler. Then they drop the marble into the tube. When it comes out of the bottom, allow the marble to roll as far as possible until it comes to a stop. Measure the distance the marble has traveled from the bottom of the tube, and the angle that the tube makes with the horizontal floor. Now move the top of the tube to a higher or lower position along the ruler and repeat the experiment. Do this several times, recording the data each time. Ask each group to come to a decision as to the "best" height for the top of the tube and the "best" angle for the tube to make with the floor in order for the marble to roll the farthest.

Extension: Repeat the experiment with different sized marbles. Does the size of the marble affect the results?

Problem 1:   The average weight of three sisters is 110 pounds. Mary, the lightest, weighs 12 pounds less than Sue, who is the heaviest. What is the weight of each sister?

Discussion: Since the average weight of the three sisters is 110 pounds, their total weight must be 330 pounds. Make a table and use the guess and test strategy.

Mary	Evelyn	Sue	
101	116	113	(no good—Sue is not the heaviest)
102	114	114	(no good—Sue is not the heaviest)
103	112	115	(OK)
104	110	116	(OK)
105	108	117	(OK)
106	106	118	(no good—Mary is not the lightest)

There are three possible answers to the problem.

Problem 2: Find the sum of the first 100 counting numbers.

Discussion: Students can add the numbers from 1 through 100 on their calculators to find the answer. However, you can approach this problem in another way, often referred to as the Gauss method of addition:

$$1 + 2 + 3 + 4 + \cdots + 97 + 98 + 99 + 100$$
$$1 + 100 = 101$$
$$2 + 99 = 101$$
$$3 + 98 = 101$$
$$\cdot \quad \cdot \quad \cdot$$
$$\cdot \quad \cdot \quad \cdot$$
$$\cdot \quad \cdot \quad \cdot$$
$$50 + 51 = 101$$

There are 50 pairs whose sum is 101, for a total of $50 \times 101 = 5{,}050$.

Teacher's Notes:

ACTIVITY 66

Title: "What Letter Should We Pick?"

Purpose and Topic: This activity will help students predict which letters occur more often than others.

Materials: An article from a current newspaper for each group of four students; a copy of Reproduction Page 48

How to Use It: On a major television show, contestants are asked to select letters to fill in the blanks in a phrase, as they attempt to identify the phrase. Why do they pick the letters they do? Ask the students which letters they would select if they were contestants on the show. Have them predict which letters they think occur most often in the English language. Record their guesses on the board. Next, distribute the newspaper article and a copy of Reproduction Page 48 to each group. Each group should select a paragraph from its article and fill in the table on Reproduction Page 48 with a tally mark each time a particular letter appears in the paragraph. Make a master list on the board or overhead projector and record the data from all the groups cumulatively. Compare the actual frequencies with the students' original guesses. The actual order in which the first few letters occur are E, T, O, A, I, N.

Extension: Tell the students that they will be asked to close their eyes and touch a pencil point to the article. Do they think that they are more likely to touch a consonant or a vowel? Why? Now have them perform the experiment. Were they correct?

Theoretically, this problem can be attacked by totaling the frequency for all the consonants and then totaling the frequency for all the vowels. The results of the experiment should approximate the ratio of these two frequencies.

Problem 1: Paul has five uncles. The oldest is age 42, and the range of their ages is 16. He noticed that both the mean and mode of the ages is 36. What are the ages of Paul's uncles? (Consider only whole number answers).

Discussion: Since the oldest is age 42 and the range is 16, the youngest must be 42 − 16 = 26. Since the mean of the five ages is 36, the total for all 5 is 180. Now, 180 − 26 − 42 = 112 for the remaining three ages. Since at least two of them must be age 36 (the mode), you have 112 − 72 = 40. Their ages are 26, 36, 36, 40, and 42.

Problem 2:   The seven members of the youth league basketball team have a median age of 14 years, a mode of 13 years, and a range of 5 years. The youngest player is 12 years old. What are the ages of the seven players? (Consider only whole numbers.)

Discussion: The median or fourth age is 14, the youngest is age 12, the oldest must be age 17.

$$\underline{12}, \ \_, \ \_, \ \underline{14}, \ \_, \ \_, \ \underline{17}$$

Since the mode is 13, you have:

$$\underline{12}, \ \underline{13}, \ \underline{13}, \ \underline{14}, \ \_, \ \_, \ \underline{17}$$

Thus, the ages must be 12, 13, 13, 14, 15, 16, and 17.

An interesting variation is to eliminate the fact that the youngest player is age 12. This permits 18 additional answers, including:

13, 13, 13, 14, 14, 15, 18   13, 13, 13, 14, 15, 15, 18
13, 13, 13, 14, 14, 16, 18   13, 13, 13, 14, 15, 16, 18
13, 13, 13, 14, 14, 17, 18   13, 13, 13, 14, 15, 17, 18
etc.

Teacher's Notes:

ACTIVITY 67   **Title:**   "Maybe Yes, Maybe No"

Purpose and Topic: This activity introduces students to the concepts of probability by asking them to decide whether events will take place.

Materials: Reproduction Page 49

How to Use It: Discuss with the students some phrases with which they are already familiar, such as "I'm sure it will," "It probably will," "There's no way it can happen," "It's unlikely," "Maybe it will," and so on. Distribute a copy of Reproduction Page 49 to each student. Introduce the sheet by explaining that sometimes people know that an event will definitely take place. Other times, people know it will not take place, and sometimes, people are not sure but know it is likely or unlikely to take place. Have the students follow the directions and complete the sheet. Then discuss their answers with the class. (*Note:* Event #4 will certainly occur with 375 people in an auditorium, since there are only 365 days in a year (or 366 in a leap year). Ask the students to answer the same question if there were 300 people in the auditorium; 250 people; 100 people.)

Extensions: You are a game-show host. You have to hide the grand prize behind door #1, door #2, door #3, or door #4. Which door are the contestants least likely to pick? To find out, give every student a piece of paper. Have them write one of the numbers from 1 to 4 on the paper, fold it, and place it in a box. Have students count the number of times each number is chosen. Discuss how this would help the game-show host.

Problem 1:   If you were to toss a coin 50 times, how many times would you expect to get "heads"? Why? Would it actually happen? Why?

Discussion: The theoretical expectation is for 1 out of 2 tosses to be heads, or 25 out of 50. However, in an actual experiment, this might not occur, due to the small number of tosses. Each time the number of tosses is increased, you should get results closer and closer to 50 percent.

Problem 2:   Michelle and her friend Antoine play a game called Add-It during recess. They toss a pair of number cubes and add the numbers that land face up. The first person who rolls a number sum five times is the winner. Which sums are possible to roll? Which sum should Michelle choose?

Discussion: The two friends can roll sums from 2 through 12. The number that should usually occur most often is 7, since there are more ways to roll a 7 than any other sum.

Sum	Ways	Number Ways
2	1	1-1
3	2	1-2, 2-1
4	3	1-3, 2-2, 3-1
5	4	1-4, 2-3, 3-2, 4-1
6	5	1-5, 2-4, 3-3, 4-2, 5-1
7	6	1-6, 2-5, 3-4, 4-3, 5-2, 6-1

Teacher's Notes:

ACTIVITY 68   **Title:** "Match Up"

Purpose and Topic: Students will perform an experiment in matching and record their results in a table. They will use their statistics to draw a conclusion about probability.

Materials: 20 cards from a standard 52-card deck (1 through 10 twice) for each group of students

How to Use It: Have the students work in groups. Each group begins by placing the cards numbered 1 through 10 in sequence, face up in a horizontal row. Next, shuffle the remaining ten cards. Now, deal one card at a time, face up, and place them directly under the other ten cards. Observe how many "matches" occur and record this in a table. Repeat this experiment a total of ten times. Students should now find the average number of matches. The mean should be close to 1.

Have the groups combine their results with those of the other groups and compute the class average. The more trials that are used, the closer the mean will be to 1. For those students who have already learned about the mode, compare the mode with the mean.

Extensions: Repeat the same experiment but use 5 cards in each deck (1 through 5), instead of the original 10. Repeat again, using the complete suit of 13 cards. The results should be approximately the same. Students should conclude that the number of cards is immaterial.

Problem 1: In a bag, there are 20 strips of paper, each with a number from 1 through 20. Judy reaches into the bag and pulls out one slip of paper. She sees that she has drawn a prime number. She puts the slip back into the bag. Ely then reaches into the bag and pulls one slip. What are the chances that the number on his slip is also a prime number? What is the chance that the number on Ely's slip will match the number on Judy's?

Discussion: Of the first 20 numbers, the following 8 are prime numbers:

   2, 3, 5, 7, 11, 13, 17, 19

The chances of Ely drawing a prime number are 8 out of 20. The chance of him matching Judy's number is 1 out of 20.

Problem 2:   Alexa's average on six math tests was 92. Her average on the first four tests was 90. If she had the same score on each of the last two tests, what were those scores?

Discussion: Alexa's average on all six tests was 92, for a total of $6 \times 92 = 552$. Her average on the first four tests was 90, for a total of $4 \times 90 = 360$.

$$552 - 360 = 192$$

She scored 96 on each of the final two tests.

Teacher's Notes:

ACTIVITY 69   **Title:**   "How's Your ESP (Extra Sensory Perception)?"

Purpose and Topic: This activity involves a fundamental concept of probability. At the same time, it affords students the opportunity to participate in an experiment, conduct a survey, and collect and organize data.

Materials: Three 3" × 5" index cards for the teacher

How to Make It: Prepare a set of three cards. On one, put a red circle; on one, a blue circle; on one, a yellow circle.

How to Use It: Shuffle the three cards and place them face down on your desk or tape them to the chalkboard. Each student should now use his or her ESP to guess the order. After the students have made their guess, poll the class. Place their responses in a table and find the ratio of guesses to the total number of guesses for each possible response.
   When all the students' data have been recorded, turn over the cards to reveal the correct order and discuss the following questions:

(a) What are the possible outcomes?
(b) How many possible outcomes are there? (Answer: 6)
(c) What is the probability of guessing the correct order? (Answer: 1/6)
(d) How close was each experimental probability (the ratio) to the theoretical probability, 1/6?

Problem 1:   Take one dime, one nickel, and one quarter, and toss all three coins in the air and let them fall to the ground. How many different ways can the three coins land? What are they?

Discussion: Each coin can land in one of two ways, either heads (H) or tails (T). Students can make a tree diagram to find the ways they can land:

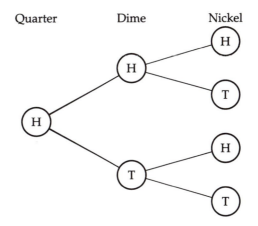

Quarter   Dime   Nickel

When the quarter lands heads up (H), there are four possibilities. Similarly, for the quarter landing tails up (T), there are also four possibilities. Thus, there are eight different ways in which the three coins can land.

Problem 2:   The letters in the word *five* are placed in a hat and three of them are picked at random. What are the chances that at least one of the letters picked is a vowel?

Discussion: The students should set up the sample space as follows:

> *five*
>
> fiv   fve
> fie   ive

All four possibilities in the sample space contain at least one vowel. Thus, there is a 100 percent chance that at least one of the letters picked is a vowel.

Problem 3:   The letters in the word *eight* are placed in a hat and three are picked at random. What are the chances that at least one of the letters picked is a vowel?

Discussion: Again, the students should set up the sample space:

> *eight*
>
> eig   egh   igh   ght
> eih   egt   igt
> eit   eht   iht

The chances of a vowel having been chosen are 9 out of 10, or 90 percent.

Teacher's Notes:

ACTIVITY 70   **Title:** "How Do You Match Up?"

Purpose and Topic: Students will conduct an experiment, develop a sample space, and determine both experimental and theoretical probabilities.

Materials: The four aces from a standard deck of playing cards for the teacher and for each student (Alternative: Students can substitute four 3" × 5" index cards with the words *spades, hearts, clubs,* and *diamonds* written on them.)

How to Use It: Shuffle the four aces and place them face down on your desk or tape them face down on the chalkboard. Have each student shuffle his or her four cards and place them face up on his or her desk. Record the order. Have each student perform this experiment a total of five times. (Do not touch your cards).

Now, together with the class, develop a table to record the class data. The table contains all 24 possible arrangements (the sample space) and columns for recording the data, as shown here. For each arrangement, the theoretical probability is 1/24.

Outcomes	Tally	Frequency	Experimental Probability	Theoretical Probability
SHCD				
SHDC				
SCHD				
SCDH				
SDHC				
SDCH				
HSCD				
HSDC				
HDSC				
HDCS				
HCSD				
HCDS				
CSHD				
CSDH				

(Continued)

Outcomes	Tally	Frequency	Experimental Probability	Theoretical Probability
CHSD				
CHDS				
CDSH				
CDHS				
DSHC				
DSCH				
DHSC				
DHCS				
DCSH				
DCHS				
TOTAL				

Poll each student for his or her five results and record them in the "Tally" column. When all the data have been recorded, complete the table entries. (The entry in the "Experimental Probability" column will be the frequency divided by the total number of trials.)

Now reveal the order for your four cards. Circle the row that shows your arrangement. How many students matched your order? How does each entry in the "Experimental Probability" column compare to 1/24?

Extension: Now create the following table:

Number of Matches	Tally	Frequency	Experimental Probability	Theoretical Probability
0				9/24
1				8/24
2				6/24
3				0/24
4				1/24

For this extension, a "match" means a correct suit in the correct position. For example:

Your Arrangement:	**S**	**H**	**C**	**D**	
	H	S	D	C	0 matches
	H	S	Ⓒ	Ⓓ	2 matches
	Ⓢ	C	H	Ⓓ	2 matches

Poll your students. How many of the students' arrangements had exactly zero matches? Exactly one match? Exactly two matches? Exactly three matches? Exactly four matches? Place tally marks on the table and complete the table. (*Note:* The theoretical probabilities were obtained by dividing the number of occurrences by the number of elements in the sample space, 24.)

(a) Compare the experimental probability to the theoretical probability.
(b) Why were there no cases of exactly three elements matching?

Problem 1: At cheerleader practice, each person has a choice of wearing a cap, a shirt, and slacks in either blue or white. Maureen was wearing a blue cap, blue shirt, and blue slacks. When Stacy arrived, what was the chance that Stacy was also wearing blue slacks? What is the chance that Stacy's uniform matched Maureen's?

Discussion: The sample space shows that there are eight possible uniform combinations:

Cap	Shirt	Slacks
B	B	B
B	B	W
B	W	B
B	W	W
W	B	B
W	B	W
W	W	B
W	W	W

The table shows that the chances Stacy and Maureen were both wearing blue slacks is 4/8, or 1/2. The chances that Stacy's uniform matched Maureen's (all blue) is 1/8.

Problem 2:   In a drawer, there are 15 black socks and 15 white socks. One night, Gina wanted to remove a pair of socks of the same color. How many socks must she remove without looking, to be sure that she has a matching pair?

Discussion: The worst-case scenario would be that the first two socks Gina picks are different. The third sock must match one of the first two. Therefore, 3 socks are required to ensure a matching pair.

Problem 3:   In a drawer, there are 15 black socks and 15 white socks. One night, Gina wanted to remove a pair of black socks. How many socks must she remove without looking, to be sure that she has a pair of black socks?

Discussion: This problem differs from the previous one in that the worst-case scenario has Gina picking 15 white socks first. She must now pick 2 additional socks to ensure a pair of black socks. Thus, 17 socks must be picked.

Teacher's Notes:

ACTIVITY 71   **Title:** "How Many in the Envelope?"

Purpose and Topic: In this activity, students will be introduced to the concept of sampling. They will be asked to predict a distribution of colored tiles or chips based on sampling techniques.

Materials: One envelope for each group of five students; an assortment of tiles or chips, some red, some blue, some green; Reproduction Page 50

How to Make It: In each envelope, place an assortment of 40 red, blue, and green chips or tiles. Some examples:

Envelope #1:   20 red, 10 blue, 10 green
Envelope #2:   13 red, 13 blue, 14 green
Envelope #3:   20 red, 20 blue, 0 green

and so on.

How to Use It: Give each student a copy of Reproduction Page 50. Have each group perform the experiment as described and answer the given questions. When the groups have completed their work, discuss their results. Make certain that the students understand the difference between *experimental (empirical)* probability and *theoretical* probability. You can have the groups repeat the experiment several more times—the experimental results should approach the theoretical results as the number of trials increases.

Extension: Have the students set up an experiment from which they can predict the color distribution of 200 M & M candies in a large box, without counting all of them.

Problem 1:   In a drawer, Lorraine had 90 golf balls, some white, some yellow, and some orange. She does not know how many of each color she has. So, she pulls 10 golf balls from the drawer at random, and finds that she has 6 white, 3 yellow, and 1 orange in her sample. How many of each color do you think she has in the drawer?

Discussion: Lorraine's sample of 10 resulted in 60 percent white, 30 percent yellow, and 10 percent orange. Based on this sample, she would expect to have 54 white golf balls, 27 yellow golf balls, and 9 orange golf balls in the drawer.

Problem 2:   Lorraine wanted to find out how many golf balls of each color she really had, so she dumped them out and counted them. She discovered she had 50 white, 30 yellow, and 10 orange. How do you account for the different answer?

Discussion: Sampling always results in an approximation, and a sample can never be depended on to give an exact answer. An illustration of this is the plus or minus variation that is always stated when a sample poll is taken.

Teacher's Notes:

ACTIVITY 72   **Title:** "Ian's Dinosaurs"

Purpose and Topic: This activity permits students to work with random numbers in a setting that is part of their real world. At the same time, they encounter some basic probability and the use of a mathematical simulation to represent an actual event.

Materials: Reproduction Page 51; one die per group of students

How to Use It: Give each group of students a copy of Reproduction Page 51 and a single die. Have them perform the experiment as shown on the Reproduction Page. Afterwards, discuss the experiment. Discuss the idea of "random numbers" and why they are designated as "random." Have them explain how this experiment is actually a simulation of the real-world situation.

Extension: The answer to question 1 as stated on Reproduction Page 51 is 501 boxes. Now, have the students answer question 1 if the store had an unlimited number of boxes of cereal. (In this case, it is impossible to obtain a numerical answer, since, theoretically, someone could continue to buy boxes with only the first five models.)

Problem 1:   The minute hand on a clock stops on a number from 1 to 60. What is the probability that the number it stopped on is divisible by both 3 and 4?

Discussion: To be divisible by both 3 and 4, the number must be divisible by 12 (the least common multiple of 3 and 4). There are five such numbers (12, 24, 36, 48, and 60). Thus, the probability is 5/60, or 1/12.

Problem 2:   A spinner stops on a number from 1 through 60. What is the probability that the number is divisible by 5 or by 6?

Discussion: There are 12 numbers divisible by 5 (5, 10, 15, 20, . . . 60) and 10 numbers divisible by 6 (6, 12, 18, 24, . . . 60) for a total of 22 numbers. But this includes 30 and 60 twice. Thus, there are 232 − 2 = 20 out of 60. The probability is 20/60, or 1/3. (*Note:* These two problems illustrate the difference between "and" and "or" problems.)

Teacher's Notes:

ACTIVITY 73   **Title:** "Over or Under?"

Purpose and Topic: This activity is an experiment to collect data that lead to an experimental probability. After calculating the theoretical probability, the experiment will show that the more cases considered, the closer the experimental and theoretical probabilities become.

Materials: Two dice (one red and one green)

How to Use It: Divide the class into pairs of students. Each pair rolls the dice and records whether the number on the green die is greater than the number on the red die. Repeat this a total of ten times. Express the result as a probability fraction—that is, the number of successes (green > red) ÷ 10. This number should now be compared to the theoretical probability. The following table shows the sample space. (The green die is the first element in each ordered pair.)

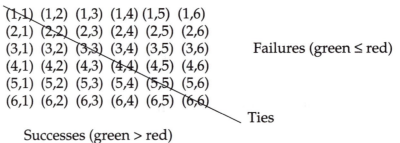

Failures (green ≤ red)

Successes (green > red)

Ties

Notice that the diagonal line (Ties) divides the sample space into three parts: green greater than red (Successes) and green equal to red and green less than red (Failures). Thus, the theoretical probability of green greater than red is 15/36.

Student pairs should now combine their results to see if the experimental probability comes closer to the theoretical as the number of trials increases.

Extension: Have students again toss the pair of dice. Add the numbers that show face up. Find the probability that this sum is greater than 7. Repeat this a total of ten times and express the results as a probability fraction. The following table shows the sample space where the sum of the dice is shown, rather than the ordered pairs:

```
                          Die #1

                  |  1   2   3   4   5   6
              ----+-------------------------
               1  |  2   3   4   5   6   7
               2  |  3   4   5   6   7   8
    Die #2     3  |  4   5   6   7   8   9
               4  |  5   6   7   8   9  10
               5  |  6   7   8   9  10  11
               6  |  7   8   9  10  11  12
```

This time, the "7" diagonal is the other major diagonal and successes are the ones below the line. Thus, the probability is, again, 15/36.

Problem 1: What is the probability of rolling an 8 with two dice?

Discussion: Use the sample space shown above. There are five 8s out of 36 possibilities, for a probability of 5/36.

Problem 2: Max is playing a game at the school math fair. He tosses a pair of dice and adds the numbers showing. If he rolls a 7, he receives a gift coupon. He rolls the dice twelve times. How many coupons would you expect Max to receive?

Discussion: There are six 7s in the sample space. Therefore, the probability of rolling a 7 is 6/36, or 1/6. With 12 tosses, Max would expect to receive two coupons. Have the students perform the experiment. Then combine their results and compare them to the actual probability.

Teacher's Notes:

ACTIVITY 74   **Title:**   "How Good Is Your Guess?"

Purpose and Topic: This activity involves students in fundamental probability, in a familiar setting.

Materials: Reproduction Page 52

How to Use It: Give each student a copy of Reproduction Page 52. Have them answer questions a through d. Now read these "answers" to the test:

1. T	**6.** F	**11.** T	**16.** F
2. T	**7.** F	**12.** T	**17.** T
3. T	**8.** T	**13.** F	**18.** F
4. F	**9.** F	**14.** F	**19.** T
5. T	**10.** T	**15.** F	**20.** F

Have the students score their papers from 1 to 20 and answer question e.

Make a graph to show the class results. On the horizontal axis, number from 1 to *n*, where *n* is the number of students in your class. Along the vertical axis, number from 1 to 20 (the number correct). Plot each student's score as a point on the graph. Draw a horizontal line through the score of 10. Theoretically, all the points should lie along this line. How close did your class approach the theoretical probability line? Now you might draw a line of best fit to see how close the experimental probability data approaches the line of theoretical probability. Discuss with the students why the two lines are not the same. That is, why don't the experimental data agree with the theoretical data?

Extension: Use the data from the T-F test to construct a bar graph. The horizontal axis represents the 20 possible scores: 1-2, 3-4, 5-6, 7-8, 9-10, and so on. The vertical axis represents the number of students who obtained this score. The tops of the bars should approximate a bell, or normal distribution, with approximately 65 percent of the scores symmetric about the 9-10 and 11-12 bars.

Problem 1:   Two cubes are numbered as follows:

Cube 1:   0 through 5
Cube 2:   0 through –5

The cubes are rolled and the face-up numbers are added. How many different sums are possible?

Discussion: Set up the sample space:

	0	1	2	3	4	5
0	0	1	2	3	4	5
−1	−1	0	1	2	3	4
−2	−2	−1	0	1	2	3
−3	−3	−2	−1	0	1	2
−4	−4	−3	−2	−1	0	1
−5	−5	−4	−3	−2	−1	0

There are eleven possible sums: −5, −4, −3, −2, −1, 0, 1, 2, 3, 4, 5.

Problem 2:   One of each number 2, 3, and 5 is written on a card and the cards are placed in a hat. Sally selects one card at a time and places them in order on the table. What is the probability that the three-digit number formed is a prime?

Discussion: There are six possible numbers:

235
325 } not prime—divisible by 5

532
352 } not prime—divisible by 2

253   not prime—divisible by 11

523   prime

The probability of the number being prime is 1/6.

Teacher's Notes:

ACTIVITY 75   **Title:**   "Fair or Unfair?"

Purpose and Topic: This activity provides practice in determining probability by constructing sample spaces. It also stimulates a discussion of the notion of fairness.

Materials: Red and black chips; a paper bag

How to Use It: Place two black chips and one red chip into a bag. Have a student select two of them without looking. If they are the same color, the student wins. If they are of different colors, the student loses. Is this a fair game? Why or why not? (The game is unfair; the probability of winning is 1/3, while the probability of losing is 2/3.)

R_1B_1 R_1B_2 $\boxed{B_1B_2}$ (Probability = 1/3)

Challenge the students to make the game fair by adding exactly one chip of either color. Which chip should they add? Intuitively, most students will suggest adding another red chip or card. This is incorrect; another black chip or card must be added. Here are the sample spaces for both situations:

Add Another Red Chip:

R_1B_1 R_1B_2 $\boxed{R_1R_2}$ R_2B_1 R_2B_2 $\boxed{B_1B_2}$ (Probability = 2/6 = 1/3)

Add Another Black Chip:

R_1B_1 R_1B_2 R_1B_3 $\boxed{B_1B_2}$ $\boxed{B_1B_3}$ $\boxed{B_2B_3}$ (Probability = 3/6 = 1/2)

Since the probability of winning is now 1/2, the game is fair if another black chip is added.

Problem 1:   Dan has three pennies in his hand. He says to Nan, "I'm going to toss these pennies. If they land all heads or all tails, I will give you a dime. Anything else, and you give me a nickel." Should Nan agree to play?

Nan reasons, "Since two of the pennies must match (either two heads or two tails), I have a 50-50 chance that the third one will match." Is this a good decision?

Discussion: The sample space is shown below:

H H H	T T T
H H T	T T H
H T H	T H T
T H H	H T T

A review reveals that Dan will win six times out of eight, while Nan will win two times out of eight. The game is not fair as Dan proposes. Nan should be paid 15¢, or 3:1, rather than 10¢, or 2:1.

Problem 2:   Mrs. Adams, the principal of the new middle school, wants one senior boy and one senior girl to be receptionists at the school entrance every morning. There are 10 girls and 20 boys in the senior class. Mrs. Adams decides to pick one girl's name from a bag with slips of paper, each with one girl's name on it. She then picks one boy's name from another bag holding slips with each boy's name. Is this method fair to each of the students? Why or why not?

Discussion: The method is not fair. Each girl has 1 chance out of 10 to be selected, whereas each boy has 1 chance out of 20.

Teacher's Notes:

CHAPTER SIX

Miscellaneous

ACTIVITY 76   **Title:**   "Squares from Squares"

Purpose and Topic: This activity involves observing patterns, squares and their areas, and some basic number theory. Students will discover that n^2 is equal to the sum of the first n odd numbers.

Materials: 1" × 1" square tiles; Reproduction Pages 53 and 54

How to Use It: Distribute a supply of tiles and a copy of Reproduction Page 53 to each student or group of students. Begin with one tile on the table. Next, have the students add as many tiles as necessary (in this case, three) to create the next smallest square. Continue the process as shown here:

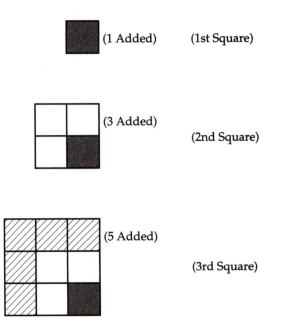

(1 Added)   (1st Square)

(3 Added)

(2nd Square)

(5 Added)

(3rd Square)

Have the students complete the next three entries in the table (trials 4, 5, and 6). (*Note:* The completed table should appear as shown.)

Column 1	Column 2	Column 3	Column 4
Trial	Number Added	Total Number of Tiles as a Sum	Total Number of Tiles
1	1	1	1
2	3	$1 + 3$	4
3	5	$1 + 3 + 5$	9
4	7	$1 + 3 + 5 + 7$	16
5	9	$1 + 3 + 5 + 7 + 9$	25
6	11	$1 + 3 + 5 + 7 + 9 + 11$	36
n	$(2n-1)$	$1 + 3 + 5 + 7 + 9 + \ldots$ (n of these)	n^2

When the students have completed their work, discuss the following with them:

(a) Describe the numbers in column 2. (These are the odd numbers.)
(b) Describe the numbers in column 4. (These are the perfect squares, or n^2.)
(c) What is the relationship between the numbers in column 1 and the numbers in column 4? (Column 4 entries are the squares of the column 1 entries.)
(d) Describe the relationship between the entries in column 1 (n) and the corresponding entries in column 2. ($2n - 1$)
(e) Describe the relationship between the entries in column 1 and the corresponding number of odd numbers in column 3. (They are equal.)
(f) State, in words, the relationship between the entries in column 3 and the corresponding entries in column 4. (The entry in column 4, n^2, equals the sum of the n entries in column 3.)

Extension: For the mathematically talented youngster, this activity can be extended to three dimensions. Start with one unit cube and determine how many additional unit cubes are needed to form the successive cubes. This can be done physically with unit cubes; however, the numbers grow so big so quickly that they make this method prohibitive. Therefore, a *symbolic simulation* is desirable. This is an excellent opportunity to show the power of mathematics. Use the table shown on Reproduction Page 54 for this extension. Guide the students through the first four trials. Have them continue through 7^3. Discuss the pattern that results. The finished table is shown here:

Column 1	Column 2	Column 3	Column 4
Trial	Number Added	*Total Number of Cubes as a Sum*	*Total Number of Cubes*
1	1	1	1
2	7	1 + 7	8
3	19	1 + 7 + 19	27
4	37	1 + 7 + 19 + 37	64
5	61	1 + 7 + 19 + 37 + 61	125
6	91	1 + 7 + 19 + 37 + 61 + 91	216
7	127	1 + 7 + 19 + 37 + 91 + 127	343
⋮	⋮		⋮
n	$\dfrac{1 + 6\,[\,n\,(n-1)\,]}{2}$		n^3

Students should be led to see the following pattern:

Trial Number	Number Added
1	$1 + 0 \cdot 6$
2	$1 + 1 \cdot 6$
3	$1 + 3 \cdot 6$
4	$1 + 6 \cdot 6$
5	$1 + 10 \cdot 6$
6	$1 + 15 \cdot 6$
7	$1 + 21 \cdot 6$

(Notice that the sequence 1, 3, 6, 10, 15, 21, . . . forms the "triangular numbers.")

Problem 1:   Ian writes his name over and over, a total of 50 times in one continuous string:

IANIANIANIANIANIAN . . .

What letter is in the 37th place?

Discussion: Some students may decide to actually write Ian's name out 50 times. Others will write it until they reach the 37th position. Students should be encouraged to discover the patterns that exist. The letter *I* occurs in positions 1, 4, 7, 10, . . . The *A* occurs in positions 2, 5, 8, 11, . . . *N* occurs in positions 3, 6, 9, 12, . . . Since *N* will occur in all positions that are multiples of 3, it will be in the 36th position. The *I* will occur in the 37th position.

Problem 2: The monorail at the amusement park starts with an empty car. At the first stop, it picks up 1 passenger. At the second stop, 3 passengers get on. At the third stop, 5 get on; 7 get on at the fourth stop, and so on. How many passengers get on at the tenth stop? If no one gets off, how many passengers will be on board the monorail after the tenth stop?

Discussion: This problem must be done in two parts and in order. Students will probably write out the ten terms of the sequence—1, 3, 5, 7, 9, 11, 13, 15, 17, 19—to arrive at their answer. Some may recognize that this is the sequence of the odd numbers, and recall the expression for the nth terms as $(2 \cdot n - 1)$. In either case, there will be 19 people getting on the monorail at the tenth stop. To solve the second part of the problem, students will either recall that the sum of the first n odd numbers is n^2, or actually sum the first ten odd numbers: $1 + 3 + 5 + 7 + 9 + 11 + 13 + 15 + 17 + 19$. The total number of people on the monorail will be 100.

Teacher's Notes:

ACTIVITY 77   **Title:** "Intersections"

Purpose and Topic: This activity is designed to provide students with experiences in recognizing patterns and expressing the relationship that exists in words and symbols.

Materials: Reproduction Page 55

How to Use It: Give all students a copy of Reproduction Page 55. Have them connect the point *furthest* from the origin on one axis to the point *closest* to the origin on the other axis. Continue in this manner. Notice that in each case, the sum of the numbers (the points connected) is a constant (2, 3, 4, . . .). Have the students draw the lines and determine the number of intersections in each of the next three cases. Record their findings in the table. Have the students determine the relationships between the number of points, the number of lines, and the number of intersections. Have them try to generalize the situation by completing the table for *n*-points. The completed table should appear as follows:

Number of Points on Each Axis	Number of Lines	Number of Intersections
1	1	0
2	2	1
3	3	3
4	4	6
5	5	10
6	6	15
n	n	$n(n-1)/2$

Extension: This activity can be extended to construct interesting and attractive displays. Students can vary the angle between the two axes, increase the number of points on each axis, and use colored pencils. They can also draw the axes on cardboard and use a needle and thread (see Activity 34).

Problem 1: The number of cells in a beaker doubles every 30 minutes. At noon, there is 1 cell in the beaker. How many cells will there be at 4:30 P.M.?

Discussion: The number of cells can be found with a table:

Time	12:00	12:30	1:00	1:30	2:00	2:30	3:00	3:30	4:00	4:30
No. Cells	1	2	4	8	16	32	64	128	256	512

There will be 512 cells at 4:30.

Problem 2:   My age now is a multiple of 5. Last year it was a multiple of 7. How old am I? How old will I be when this happens next?

Discussion: Make a table:

Age Now	5	10	15	20	25	30	35	40	45	50
Last Year	4	9	14	19	24	29	34	39	44	49

The table reveals that I am either 15 or 50 years old.

Some students may recognize that this problem involves the least common multiple of 5 and 7—namely, 35. Once the initial set is determined, the next occurrence will be 35 years later, at age 50 and then again at age 85.

Teacher's Notes:

ACTIVITY 78   **Title:**   "Coded Messages"

Purpose and Topic: This activity provides students with an opportunity to practice using a metric ruler.

Materials: Reproduction Page 56

How to Use It: Give each student a copy of Reproduction Page 56. The student must answer the question "What Will Happen to the Inchworm When We 'Go Metric'?" by finding the coded message. Each letter is represented by one or more measurements on the given "ruler." Measurements are provided in various metric units. The ruler is shown in centimeters. Students find the correct position for each letter and mark it directly above its position. The first letter, *U* has been done for them. The final message should read: "IT'LL BECOME A LITERBUG":

```
   I T ' L L   B E C O M E   A   L I T E R B U G
```

Extension: You can create sheets similar to this one, using the results of arithmetic operations on fractions, decimals, and so on. The same kind of activity can be used with an English unit ruler, as well. Keep the message brief, and the "cornier" the better.

Problem 1:   Dan is putting a Mickey Mouse border around the baby's room. He needs 50 meters of border altogether. Amy gave him 15 meters that she had left over. The border comes in 5-meter lengths. How many additional lengths does Dan have to buy?

Discussion:

   50m − 15m = 35m
   35m ÷ 5m = 7m

Dan must buy 7 additional lengths.

Problem 2:   At the end of the race, Carol was 50 meters ahead of Linda. Theresa was 10 meters behind Margaret. Linda was 30 meters ahead of Theresa. Who won the race? Who finished second? Third? Fourth?

Discussion: The first clue places Carol 50 meters ahead of Linda. The third clue places Theresa 30 meters behind Linda. The second clue places

Theresa 10 meters behind Margaret. Thus, Carol was first, Linda was second, Margaret was third, and Theresa was fourth

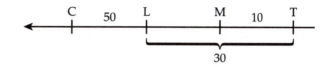

Teacher's Notes:

ACTIVITY 79   **Title:**   "Can You Solve These 'Equations'?"

Purpose and Topic: This is a puzzle activity that requires students to replace a letter with the word that makes the statement true.

Materials: Reproduction Page 57

How to Use It: Give each student a copy of Reproduction Page 57. The first "equation" is done for them. The answers are as follows:

1. Sides in a Hexagon
2. Degrees in a Circle
3. Pounds in a Ton
4. Innings in a Baseball Game
5. Degrees at Which Water Boils
6. Inches in a Yard
7. Degrees in the Angles of a Triangle
8. Grams in a Kilogram
9. Quarts in a Gallon
10. Days in a Year

Extension: Have the students create their own puzzle statements. Ask the rest of the class to try to decipher them.

Problem 1:   Four classes in the seventh grade collected 1,200 aluminum cans in a scrap drive. The number of cans collected by each class differed by 100. How many cans did each class collect?

Discussion: Algebraically, the problem can be solved as follows:

$$\begin{aligned}
\text{First class} &= x\\
\text{Second class} &= x + 100\\
\text{Third class} &= x + 200\\
\text{Fourth class} &= x + 300\\
x + x + 100 + x + 200 + x + 300 &= 1{,}200\\
4x + 600 &= 1{,}200\\
4x &= 600\\
x &= 150
\end{aligned}$$

The classes collected 150, 250, 350, and 450 cans, respectively.

For those students who are not able to use algebra, the problem can be solved by guess and test. Since the average number collected is 300 cans, students should try numbers below and above this average.

Problem 2: The Cougars played a 48-game schedule. They won 10 more games than they lost. They tied 8 games. How many games did they win?

Discussion:

48 games − 8 ties = 40 games

By guess and test, they won 25 games and lost 15.
An alternate solution would be to use the power of algebra.

Teacher's Notes:

ACTIVITY 80   **Title:**   "Mathematical Word Search"

Purpose and Topic: This activity is designed to challenge the ability of students to recognize and spell mathematical terms.

Materials: Reproduction Pages 58 and 59

How to Use It: Distribute a copy of Reproduction Page 58 to each student or group of students. Have them draw an oval around each of the 21 mathematical terms hidden in the array. Remind them that words can be hidden vertically, horizontally, diagonally, forward, or backward. They may even find one word hidden inside another or in more than one place. (For example, the word *angle* is hidden inside both rec*tangle* and tri*angle*.) Any one letter may be found in more than one word. You may wish to do one or two to show the class how the puzzle is done. The answer key is shown here:

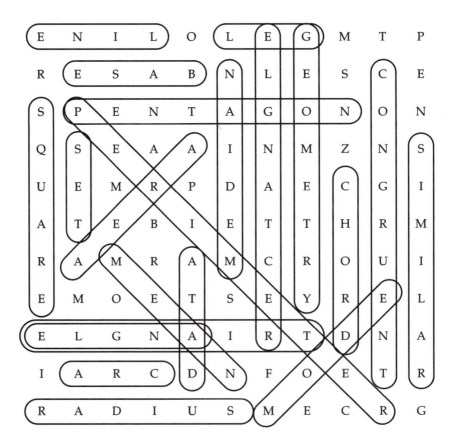

Extensions: Reproduction Page 59 contains an array that conceals metric words and abbreviations. It can be used as just discussed. However, the hidden words and abbreviations are not given.

You might also wish to create your own word search for other terms, such as *number operations, algebraic terms,* and so on, or have the students create their own.

Problem 1: The students in the school Crossing Patrol are going to the circus. There are more than 10 but fewer than 15 students in the group. Each student paid the same dollar amount, and the total was $221. How many students went on the trip? How much did each pay?

Discussion: Look for the factors of 221, one of which must lie between 10 and 15. The number 221 has only two factors, 17 and 13. Since there were fewer than 15 students, the answer to the problem is 13 students, each of whom paid $17.

Problem 2: There are 20 Girl Scouts walking single file through the woods. Two mosquitoes are watching them from a pond. The first mosquito decides to bite every odd-numbered Scout in the line. The second mosquito then bites all Scouts whose position in the line is a multiple of 3. How many Scouts were not bitten? How many were bitten twice?

Discussion: Make a table:

Mosquito #1	1	3	5	7	9	11	13	15	17	19
Mosquito #2		3		6	9		12	15		18

All the even-numbered Scouts except 6, 12, and 18 were not bitten. Scouts 3, 9, and 15 were bitten twice.

Teacher's Notes:

ACTIVITY 81   **Title:**   "Word Values"

Purpose and Topic: This activity provides the students with an interesting setting for practice in adding money.

Materials: Reproduction Page 60

How to Make It: Prepare a dollar assignment chart. You can place the chart on the board or distribute a copy of Reproduction Page 60 to each student.

How to Use It: This activity can be done alone or in small groups. Begin by using Table 1 on Reproduction Page 60. Students are asked to find the dollar value for a variety of words. For example, the class might begin by finding the value for some common words such as the name of the school, the value of an animal (such as the word *cat*, *alligator*, etc.), and so on. They might then be asked to find the student with the most (or least) expensive first name or family name. Connections can also be made to social studies by looking for the most (least) expensive name of a city in your state or the most (least) expensive state.

   After the students have had practice in using the table of dollar values, the activity should be extended by using the table of dollars and cents (Table 2 on Reproduction Page 60) and then to the table of mixed cent values (Table 3).

Extension: The inverse problem should also be undertaken. That is, find a name in the class with a specific value or an animal name with a specific value.

Problem 1:   There is a game at the County Fair called Gum Ball Back. You throw chips into a slot and the machine returns gum balls. Maury played the game. The table shows the number of gum balls he received each time. If Maury puts in 20 chips, how many gum balls will he get? If Maury gets 96 gum balls, how many chips did he put in?

Discussion:

Input	3	8	11	12	. . .	20	. . .	?
Output	0	15	24	27	. . .	?	. . .	96

   Notice that the outputs are all multiples of 3. The pattern can be seen by inserting 9 and 10 in the Input row. These lead to 18 and 21, respectively, in the Output row. As the input increases by 1, the output increases by 3. The rule for the gum ball machine is $3(n - 3)$. Thus, for 20 chips, the output is 51; for an output of 96, the input is 35.

Problem 2:   Orange lollipops are sold in packs of three. Lime lollipops are sold in packs of five. Henry bought 42 orange and lime lollipops combined. How many packs of orange could he have bought?

Discussion: The problem is solved by guess and test, with a table:

Orange (3)	14	9	4
Lime (5)	0	3	6

Henry could have bought 4, 9, or 14 packs of orange lollipops.

Teacher's Notes:

ACTIVITY 82   **Title:**   "Which Doesn't Belong and Why?"

Purpose and Topic: This activity provides students with an opportunity to identify commonalities. Since the items may fit into more than one category, answers may vary. Students will develop their communication skills as they explain "why" they selected the item they did.

Materials: Reproduction Page 61

How to Use It: Divide the class into groups of three or four students. Give each group a copy of Reproduction Page 61. The page contains 15 sets, each of which lists four items. Students are to decide which item they feel does not belong with the rest. They must also be prepared to give a reason for their choice. For example, for number 1, some students may select 20 as the item that does not belong, since it is the only one not divisible by 9. Other students might select 9 as the one that does not belong, since it is the only one-digit numeral in the set. Others might select 9 as different, since it is the only odd number. All of these choices are correct, as long as the group presents a valid reason for their choice. Discuss all the choices with the entire class. Some possible selections might be:

1. 9—the only single-digit number; or
   9—the only odd number; or
   20—the only number not divisible by 9.
2. $\sqrt{7}$ —the only irrational number.
3. Hockey—the only game not played with a ball.
4. 15—the only nonperfect square; or
   49—the only one not divisible by 3.
5. Orange—the only color not a primary color.
6. Pentagon—the only one that is not a quadrilateral.
7. 8106—the only one that is not a palindrome (read the same backward and forward); or
   747—the only one not a four-digit numeral.
8. A—the only letter that is not also a Roman numeral; or
   D—the only letter not made with only straight lines.
9. 81—the only one that is not a perfect cube; or
   8—the only numeral without a 1.
10. 33 →66—the only one not in the ratio of 2 to 3.
11. 1931—the only one not a memorable date in U.S. history; or
    1931—the only odd number in the set.
12. New York—the only one that is not a state capital.
13. 2 feet 10 inches—the one that is not equivalent to 40 inches.
14. 3—the only single digit numeral; or
    57—the only one that is not a prime number.
15. New England—the only one that is not a state.

Extension: Have the groups make up their own "Which Doesn't Belong and Why?" sets. Be certain that they make sets with more than one single choice a possibility.

Problem 1: Tickets for the Bouncing Boulders concert go on sale at exactly 9:30 A.M. The guards admit only a fixed number of people every five minutes. At 9:00, the first person got in line. At 9:05, 1 more person got in line. At 9:10, 2 people got in line. Every five minutes, as many people joined the line as were already on the line. How many people joined the line at 9:30? How many people were now in line as the box office opened?

Discussion: Make a table:

Time	Number Added	Number on Line
9:00	1	1
9:05	1	2
9:10	2	4
9:15	4	8
9:20	8	16
9:25	16	32
9:30	32	64

There were 32 people joining the line at 9:30. There were 64 people in the line.

Problem 2: Mrs. Taylor asked her class to add two positive numbers. Barbara subtracted them instead, and got 4 as her answer. Jerry multiplied them instead, and got 221 as his answer. What should they have gotten?

Discussion: Since the product was 221, you are looking for two factors of 221 that differ by 4. The number 221 only has two factors—namely, 13 and 17. These are the two numbers. Barbara and Jerry should have gotten 30 as their answer.

Teacher's Notes:

ACTIVITY 83   **Title:**   "Mind-Reading Cards"

Purpose and Topic: Students are always interested in how computers work. This activity will offer some insight into this type of logic, through the concept of "yes-no" or "0-1" reasoning. In addition, it provides some introduction into number bases other than 10—namely, base 2.

Materials: Reproduction Page 62; scissors

How to Make It: Give each student a copy of Reproduction Page 62. Have all students cut out the six cards. (For a more permanent deck, paste the cut out cards onto cardboard or poster-board and laminate them.)

How to Use It: Ask one student to select any number from 1 through 63 and tell it to everyone else, but not to you. Ask him or her to tell you on which of the six cards his or her number appears. After this is done, you can tell the student's number simply by finding the sum of the first number on each card that the student has selected.

   After repeating this "mind-reading trick" a few times, the explanation of why it works should be discussed with the class. Look at this table with some of these numbers expressed in base 2:

Decimal	$32(2^5)$	$16(2^4)$	$8(2^3)$	$4(2^2)$	$2(2^1)$	1
1	0	0	0	0	0	1
2	0	0	0	0	1	0
3	0	0	0	0	1	1
4	0	0	0	1	0	0
5	0	0	0	1	0	1
6	0	0	0	1	1	0
7	0	0	0	1	1	1
8	0	0	1	0	0	0
9	0	0	1	0	0	1
10	0	0	1	0	1	0
11	0	0	1	0	1	1
12	0	0	1	1	0	0
13	0	0	1	1	0	1
14	0	0	1	1	1	0
15	0	0	1	1	1	1
16	0	1	0	0	0	0

Decimal	$32(2^5)$	$16(2^4)$	$8(2^3)$	$4(2^2)$	$2(2^1)$	1
17	0	1	0	0	0	1
.	.	.	.	.	.	.
43	1	0	1	0	1	1

All the numbers on Card I (the odd numbers) have a 1 in the units or 1s column. All the numbers on Card II (2, 3, 6, 7, 10, 11, 14, 15, ...) have a 1 in the 2s column (they may have a 1 somewhere else, as well). All the numbers on Card III have a 1 in the 4s column, and so on. You can find the student's number by adding the headings of those columns in which the 1s appear. These are the same as the first number on each card. For example, 17 appears on Card I and Card V. In base 2, 17 would be written as 10001. You would add 16 + 1 to get 17. Similarly, 43 appears on Card I, Card II, Card IV, and Card VI. Thus, you would add 32 + 8 + 2 + 1 = 43. (In base 2, 43 is written as 101011). The cards are really a "computer" in base 2.

Extension: To extend the deck to include all the numbers from 1 through 127, you would need one more card (2^6, or 64). In addition, you would have to represent all the numbers from 64 through 127 in base 2, in order to place them on the appropriate original cards. For instance, 103 in base 2 would be 1(64) + 1(32) + 0(16) + 0(8) + 1(4) + 1(2) + 1, or 1100111 in base 2. The number 103 would appear on Cards I, II, III, VI, and VII (the new card). This new card would not contain any numbers smaller than 64.

Problem 1: Mitchell has a wooden box in which he stores miniature clay flower pots. When the box has 30 pots in it, it weighs 330 ounces. When it has 15 pots in it, it weighs 180 ounces. Every pot weighs the same. What is the weight of the box when it is empty?

Discussion:

30 pots + box = 330 ounces
15 pots + box = 180 ounces

Subtracting, you will find that 15 pots = 150 ounces, or each pot = 10 ounces.

30(10 ounces) + box = 330 ounces
300 ounces + box = 330 ounces
box = 30 ounces

Problem 2:   Anita, Billy, Charlene, and David each measured the length of a room that is 30' long, using his or her shoes as the unit of measure. Here are the sizes of their shoes:

Anita = 8 1/2"   Charlene = 10 1/2"
Billy = 9 1/2"   David = 11 1/2"

Their teacher called on the student whose measurement was closest to 35 shoe lengths. Who did the teacher call on?

Discussion:

30' = 360"
360 ÷ 11 1/2 = 31.3
360 ÷ 10 1/2 = 34.2

Charlene's shoes measured closest to 35 shoe units.
    An alternate solution is to compare the actual lengths of 35 shoe units for the two largest:

35 × 10 1/2 = 367.5
35 × 11 1/2 = 402.5

Charlene's measure is closest to 360 inches.

Teacher's Notes:

ACTIVITY 84   **Title:** "The Golden Ratio"

Purpose and Topic: The Greek philosopher and mathematician, Pythagoras, wrote that the "Golden Ratio" (approximately 8:5) appears everywhere. The "Golden Rectangle" is so named because the ratio of the longer side to the shorter side is the same 8:5. In fact, its proportions are supposedly the most pleasing to the eye. This activity provides the students with an opportunity to examine various objects and parts of the human body to determine if this golden ratio is present.

Materials: Reproduction Page 63; tape measures or yardsticks; calculators; rectangular objects such as index cards, sheets of paper, the cover of a textbook, a window pane, a picture frame, and so on.

How to Use It: Divide the class into groups of four or five students. Give each group a copy of Reproduction Page 63, a tape measure or yardstick, several of the rectangular objects, and a calculator. Have the group perform the measurements asked for on the Reproduction Page, convert its results into decimal form, and then draw whatever conclusions possible. Ask the groups if any of the rectangular shapes are particularly "pleasing" to their eye. Do these come close to the Golden Rectangle?

Next, have the students perform the measurements on the second part of the page and compute the ratios in decimal form. Again, ask them to draw conclusions. This time, too, most of their ratios should be approximately 8:5, or the Golden Ratio. Point out that this ratio is still being used in buildings, paintings, and so on.

Extension: The numbers in the Fibonacci sequence 1, 1, 2, 3, 5, 8, 13, 21, 34, 55, 89, 144, 233, . . . are also related to the Golden Ratio. If you set up the ratio of two successive terms (i.e., 1/1, 2/1, 3/2, 5/3, 8/5, 13/8, 21/13, 34/21, . . .) you will find that these ratios approach the golden ratio. In fact, at 233/144, the ratio will be 1.6181, quite close to the golden 8:5.

Problem 1:   John rode his bike 4/5 of the way to the ballpark in 28 minutes. At this same rate, how long will the entire trip take him?

Discussion: Set up a proportion as follows:

$$\frac{4}{5} = \frac{28}{x}$$
$$4x = 140$$
$$x = 35$$

The trip will take 35 minutes.

A student without an algebra background can reason as follows. Since 4/5 of the trip take 28 minutes, 1/5 of the trip will take 7 minutes, and the entire trip (5/5) will take 5 × 7 or 35 minutes.

Problem 2:   *Primetime* is defined as a day of the year when the number of the month and the number of the day are both primes. Thus, May 7 is an example of primetime (i.e., 5/7). What would be the first and the last primetimes of a year?

Discussion: The only months that contain primetimes would be February (2), March (3), May (5), July (7), and November (11). Thus, the earliest primetime would be February 2 (2/2) and the last primetime would be November 29 (11/29).

Teacher's Notes:

ACTIVITY 85   **Title:**   "Mobius Strip"

Purpose and Topic: This activity provides students with an example of a "one-sided" figure—that is, a figure in which it is possible to draw a single, continuous line on both sides of a strip of paper without crossing over an edge.

Materials: Strips of paper approximately 15 to 20 inches long and about 4 inches wide; scissors; tape; crayons

How to Make It: Each student takes one strip of paper. Mark one end AB and the other CD as shown here:

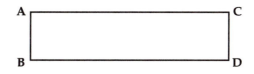

Tape the ends of the strip together so that A falls on C and B falls on D. Do *not* twist the strip of paper before taping. Take a second strip of paper. This time, give it a twist before taping, so that A falls on D and B falls on C. (This is called a *Mobius Strip*, after the German mathematician, August Mobius.)

How to Use It: Have the students color one side of the first strip without crossing an edge. Discuss how many "sides" this loop has and why. (There are two sides, since it is necessary to cross an edge if one wishes to color the other side.) Now, have the students draw one continuous line, midway between the edges, until they return to the starting point. Next, have them cut along this line. They obtain two loops when done. Have them describe what happens.

Take the second strip. Repeat the experiment. Notice that the entire strip can now be colored without crossing over an edge. Now, have the students cut along a line that they drew midway between the edges (as shown). What happens this time? Discuss the results.

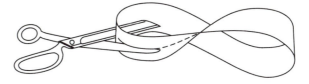

(Students will end up with a single, large band.)

Extension: Have the students make another Mobius Strip. This time, they should begin to cut along a line approximately 1/3 of the way from one edge and continue cutting until they arrive back at their starting point. Have the students describe what has happened.

Problem 1:   Represent the numbers from 0 through 10 using only four 4s. The symbols $+$, $-$, $\times$, $\div$, $\sqrt{}$, or a fraction bar may be used.

Discussion: There are many answers possible. Be certain to discuss them all with the class. Here is one possible set:

$0 = (4 + 4) - (4 + 4)$ $6 = [(4 + 4) \div 4] + 4$
$1 = (4 \div 4) \times (4 \div 4)$ $7 = 4 + 4 - 4/4$
$2 = (4 \div 4) + (4 \div 4)$ $8 = 4 + 4 + 4 - 4$
$3 = (4 + 4 + 4) \div 4$ $9 = 4 + 4 + (4 \div 4)$
$4 = 4 + 4 - \sqrt{4} - \sqrt{4}$ $10 = 4 \times 4 - 4 - \sqrt{4}$
$5 = [(4 \times 4) + 4] \div 4$

Problem 2:   Represent the numbers from 0 through 9 using exactly three 3s. The symbols $+$, $-$, $\times$, $\div$, $\sqrt{}$, and ! may be used.

Discussion: Again, there may be more than one answer for each. Here is one possible set of answers:

$0 = 3(3 - 3)$ $5 = 3! - (3/3)$
$1 = 3! \div (3 + 3)$ $6 = \sqrt{3 \times 3} + 3$
$2 = 3 - (3 \div 3)$ $7 = 3! + (3 \div 3)$
$3 = 3 \times 3 \div 3$ $8 = (3!/3) + 3!$
$4 = 3 + (3 \div 3)$ $9 = 3^3 \div 3$

Teacher's Notes:

ACTIVITY 86   **Title:** "The Seven Bridges of Koenigsberg"

Purpose and Topic: In this activity, students will be introduced to networks, odd and even vertices, and traversability.

Materials: Reproduction Pages 64, 65, and 66; colored pencils

How to Make It: Distribute a copy of Reproduction Pages 64, 65, and 66 to the students. Give each student several different colored pencils.

How to Use It: Follow these steps:

(a) Begin by telling the following story to the class.

The town of Koenigsberg in old Germany was famous for its seven bridges. Six of these ran from each bank of the Preger River to two islands, while the seventh bridge connected the two islands (see Reproduction Page 64 and the following figure).

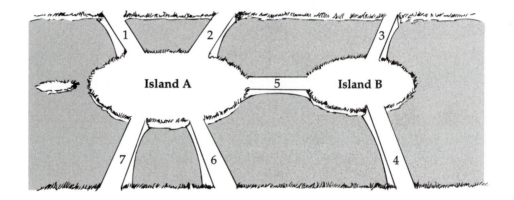

The story tells that the mayor of the town offered a great prize to anyone who could walk across each of the seven bridges one time only, never recrossing any of the bridges. Ask the students if they can do it. Tell them to use their pencils to attempt to draw a continuous path across all seven bridges without crossing any of them more than once. Can it be done? (No.)

(b) Leonard Euler, a Swiss mathematician of the 1700s, became interested in this problem. He discovered some rules about what are called *networks*. A network is a continuous figure made up of a group of lines called *arcs* and a series of dots called *corners* or *vertices*.

(c) Have your students examine the seven networks shown on Reproduction Page 65. A vertex is *even* if an even number of arcs emanate from it. A vertex is *odd* if an odd number of arcs emanate from it.

For each network on Reproduction Page 65, have the students try to trace it with one continuous line that never retraces itself or goes over any part of itself. Keep track of their work on the Data Sheet shown on Reproduction Page 66. A finished Data Sheet will look like this:

Network	Number of EVEN Vertices	Number of ODD Vertices	Can It Be Traced in One Continuous Line?
1	4	2	Yes
2	1	4	No
3	4	0	Yes
4	4	2	Yes
5	3	2	Yes
6	2	4	No
7	10	0	Yes

The data should lead them to the following conclusions:

(a) A network can be traveled in exactly one trip if it contains only even vertices.

(b) A network can be traveled in exactly one trip if it contains exactly two odd vertices.

Now, have the students repeat the original problem as a network:

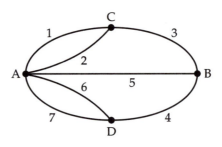

Points A and B represent the two islands; C and D represent the river banks. Have them use their rules to see if the network can be traveled in exactly one trip. (It cannot, since all the vertices are odd.)

Extension: Have the students add an eighth bridge to the original problem wherever they wish. Can they travel through this network without going back over any bridge? Have several students show their figures and solutions to this "new" problem.

Problem 1: Mrs. Cannon has to replace some broken glass panes in her kitchen window. The window is a square and is made up of smaller square panes of glass. When she got to the store, she said to the sales person, "I can't remember how many small panes I need, but I know it's fewer than 5. Also, I remember that exactly 13 of the smaller panes in the window aren't broken." How many small panes does Mrs. Cannon need?

Discussion: Since the large window is a square and each of the small panes is also a square, the number of smaller panes must be 1, 4, 9, 16, 25, ... The condition that 13 are not broken and she needs fewer than 5 limits the number of panes in the original window to 16, and she needs to buy 3 small panes.

Problem 2: A certain outlet store has an interesting pricing system. When an item is put on the sale rack, the regular selling price is reduced by 25 percent. Each week the item remains on the rack, it is reduced by another 25 percent. Janet bought a dress during the fourth week it was on the rack. The dress originally cost $96. How much did Janet pay for the dress?

Discussion: Make a table:

Week	---	1	2	3	4
Price	$96	$72	$54	$40.50	$30.38

Janet spent $30.38 for the dress.

Teacher's Notes:

ACTIVITY 87   **Title:**   "The Map-Coloring Problem"

Purpose and Topic: In this activity, students will discover the four-color theorem of topology—namely, that any map can be colored with no more than four different colors.

Materials: Reproduction Page 67; crayons

How to Use It: Provide each student or group of students with a copy of Reproduction Page 67 and at least five or six different colored crayons. Begin by discussing with the class the necessity for coloring adjacent areas on maps with distinct colors. Adjacent areas are considered to be those areas having a boundary in common. A common point is not considered a common boundary. Since color printing is a very expensive process, map-makers try to use as few colors as possible. Now ask the students to color the "maps" on Reproduction Page 67 with as few colors as possible. (*Note:* The first two maps require only two colors; the rest require four colors.) Have several students show how they colored their maps. Discuss the number of different colors each map requires.

As yet, no one has ever been able to draw a map that requires more than four colors. Have the students draw their own maps, making them as complicated as they wish. Exchange maps with a neighbor and color the maps with as few colors as possible. No map should require more than four colors.

Problem 1:   In a standard deck of 52 playing cards, how many cards must William select to be certain he has an ace?

Discussion: Examine the worst-case scenario—namely, William selects 48 cards without getting an ace. Thus, the 49th card assures him of picking an ace.

Problem 2:   Four friends went into the local ice cream shop and each ordered a different flavor: vanilla, chocolate, strawberry, and butter pecan. Albert is allergic to chocolate. Caren's husband ordered vanilla. Caren cannot eat nuts because they stick in her braces. Bob handed the chocolate cone to his wife, Denise. Who ordered each flavor?

Discussion: Use a matrix and examine each clue in turn.

	Vanilla	Chocolate	Strawberry	Butter Pecan
Albert	YES	X	X	X
Bob	X	X	X	YES
Caren	X	X	YES	X
Denise	X	YES	X	X

Albert ordered vanilla, Bob ordered butter pecan, Caren ordered strawberry, and Denise ordered chocolate.

Teacher's Notes:

CHAPTER SEVEN

Reproduction Pages

REPRODUCTION PAGE 1

Student's Name _____ Date _____

TARGET 500 BOARD

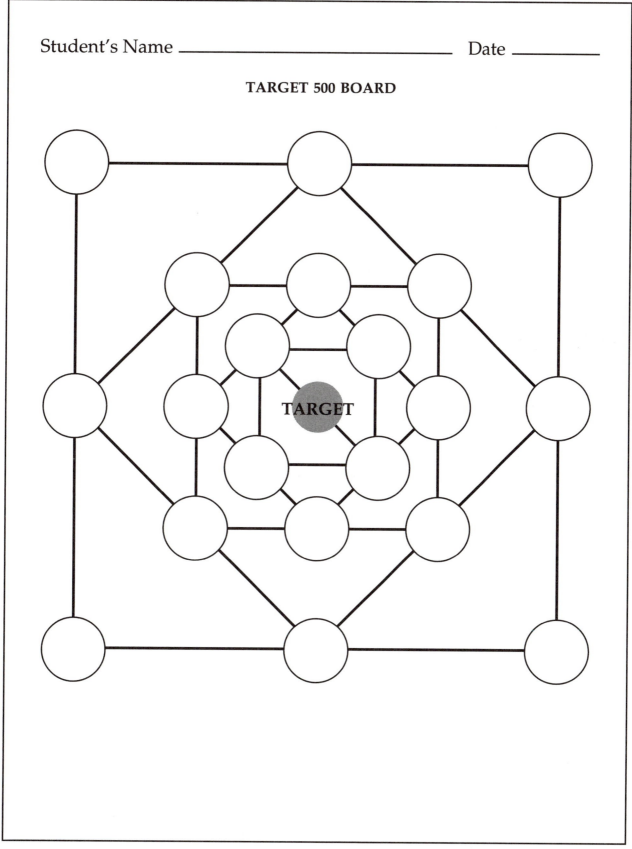

Student's Name _____ Date _____

MAGIC SQUARE

Directions: Use the numbers from 1 through 9 to complete the magic square shown below. In a magic square, each row, column, and both diagonals have the same sum.

		6
	5	
4		2

REPRODUCTION PAGE 3

Student's Name _____ Date _____

TARGET 0 BOARD

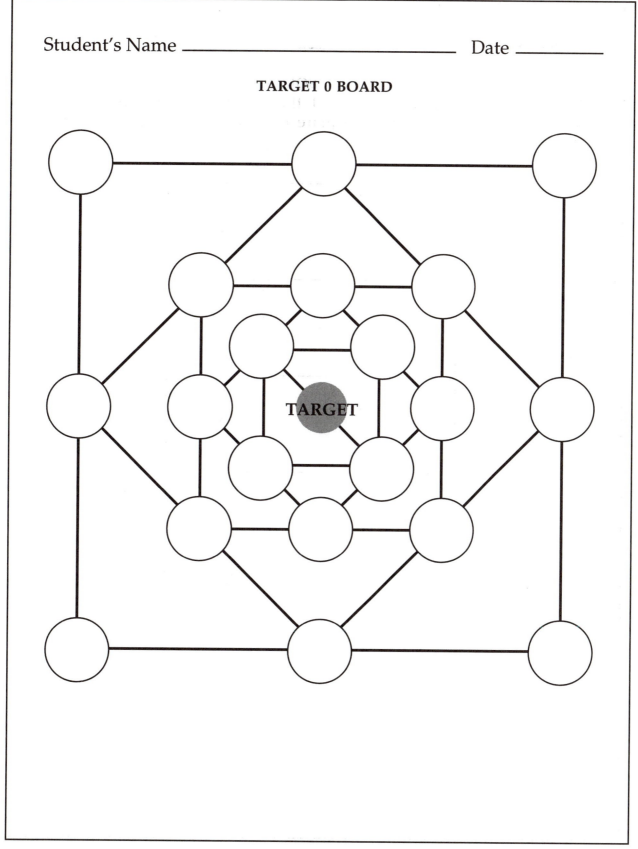

Student's Name _____ Date _____

ADDITION/SUBTRACTION SLIDE RULE

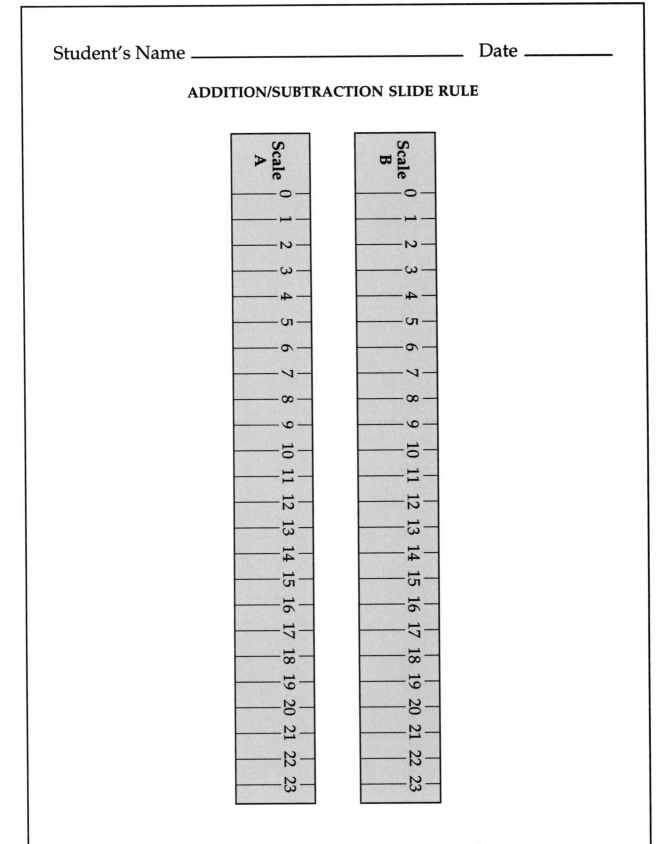

REPRODUCTION PAGE 5

Student's Name _____ Date _____

NAPIER RODS

Index	1	2	3	4	5	6	7	8	9	0
1	0/1	0/2	0/3	0/4	0/5	0/6	0/7	0/8	0/9	0/0
2	0/2	0/4	0/6	0/8	1/0	1/2	1/4	1/6	1/8	0/0
3	0/3	0/6	0/9	1/2	1/5	1/8	2/1	2/4	2/7	0/0
4	0/4	0/8	1/2	1/6	2/0	2/4	2/8	3/2	3/6	0/0
5	0/5	1/0	1/5	2/0	2/5	3/0	3/5	4/0	4/5	0/0
6	0/6	1/2	1/8	2/4	3/0	3/6	4/2	4/8	5/4	0/0
7	0/7	1/4	2/1	2/8	3/5	4/2	4/9	5/6	6/3	0/0
8	0/8	1/6	2/4	3/2	4/0	4/8	5/6	6/4	7/2	0/0
9	0/9	1/8	2/7	3/6	4/5	5/4	6/3	7/2	8/1	0/0

Student's Name ———————————————— Date ————

FACTOR GAME

Directions: Players alternate turns. When it is his or her turn, each player selects a number from the array for his or her score. That number is then crossed out from the array. The other player takes the factors of those numbers that remain and enters them for his or her score. The roles are then reversed and play continues.

1	2	3	4	5	6	7	8	9	10
11	12	13	14	15	16	17	18	19	20
21	22	23	24	25	26	27	28	29	30
31	32	33	34	35	36	37	38	39	40
41	42	43	44	45	46	47	48	49	50

REPRODUCTION PAGE 7

Student's Name ——————————————— Date ————

SCORE WITH 4 GAME BOARD

1	
2	
3	
4	
5	
6	
7	
8	
9	
10	
11	
12	
13	
14	
15	
16	
17	
18	
19	
20	
21	
22	
23	
24	
25	

Student's Name _____ Date _____

GRID FOR EQUATION SEARCH

Directions: You are to discover any true equations within the grid by placing the appropriate operational symbols and the equal sign. Parentheses may be used, and a number may occur in more than one equation. One has already been done for you.

9	6	3	81	(42 ÷ 7 = 6)	19	23
45	2	3	27	8	6	8	25	8
5	7	18	3	5	1	14	7	15
21	4	4	9	6	14	3	11	5
58	7	4	28	2	15	2	9	75
3	18	7	2	5	10	8	3	12
36	9	49	14	2	28	42	7	63
7	6	7	36	9	4	50	3	11
32	54	6	9	8	3	6	5	12

REPRODUCTION PAGE 9

Student's Name _____ Date _____

PUT IN THE SIGNS

Directions: Insert the proper operation signs to make both the horizontal rows and vertical columns true statements. Work from left to right and from top to bottom.

7		2		5	=	10
	■		■		■	
10		5		1	=	3
	■		■		■	
3		6		3	=	6
=	■	=	■	=	■	=
0		1		1	=	1

6		3		6	=	8
	■		■		■	
12		2		8	=	3
	■		■		■	
2		3		5	=	10
=	■	=	■	=	■	=
20		9		3	=	14

REPRODUCTION PAGE 10

Student's Name _____ Date _____

SIEVE OF ERATOSTHENES

	2	3	4	5	6	7	8	9	10
11	12	13	14	15	16	17	18	19	20
21	22	23	24	25	26	27	28	29	30
31	32	33	34	35	36	37	38	39	40
41	42	43	44	45	46	47	48	49	50
51	52	53	54	55	56	57	58	59	60
61	62	63	64	65	66	67	68	69	70
71	72	73	74	75	76	77	78	79	80
81	82	83	84	85	86	87	88	89	90
91	92	93	94	95	96	97	98	99	100

REPRODUCTION PAGE 11

Student's Name _____ Date _____

CONSTRUCTING PRIMES AND COMPOSITES

Directions: Use the appropriate number of tiles to form rectangles. Record your findings in the table below. Here are the rules:

1. Tiles must lie flat on the table.
2. Adjacent tiles must share a common edge.

Number of Tiles	How Many Different Rectangles?	Dimensions	Area	Figure
2	1	1 × 2	2	
3				
4	2	1 × 4 2 × 2	4	
5				
6				
7				
8				
9				
10				
11				
12				

1. List the numbers for which you were only able to form one rectangle.

   These numbers are called *prime numbers*. A prime number is a number that has only one factor pair: itself and 1.

2. What would be the next prime number? _____
   Do you see any pattern?

(Continued)

3. Do you think that this list will ever end? Why or why not?

4. List the numbers for which you were able to form more than one rectangle.

These numbers are called *composite numbers*. Composite numbers have more than one factor pair.

A prime number may be considered as any number for which only one rectangle can be formed. A composite number is any number for which more than one rectangle can be formed.

REPRODUCTION PAGE 12

Student's Name _____ Date _____

COMPU CARD

C	O	M	P	U
		FREE		

REPRODUCTION PAGE 13

Student's Name _____ Date _____

COMPU MASTER CARD

Number Pair	+	–	×	÷

REPRODUCTION PAGE 14

Student's Name _____ Date _____

MULTIPLO

24 3 18 6	27 9 30 2	14 8 16 3	18 5 40 4
25 7 30 6	36 4 18 7	28 8 28 3	24 2 12 7
20 3 40 6	16 4 14 5	30 4 15 7	48 5 16 5
32 2 24 8	16 3 21 8	30 2 60 4	24 9 40 5
27 3 18 6	42 4 14 8	28 7 36 7	18 7 26 9

Student's Name _____ Date _____

MULTIPLO

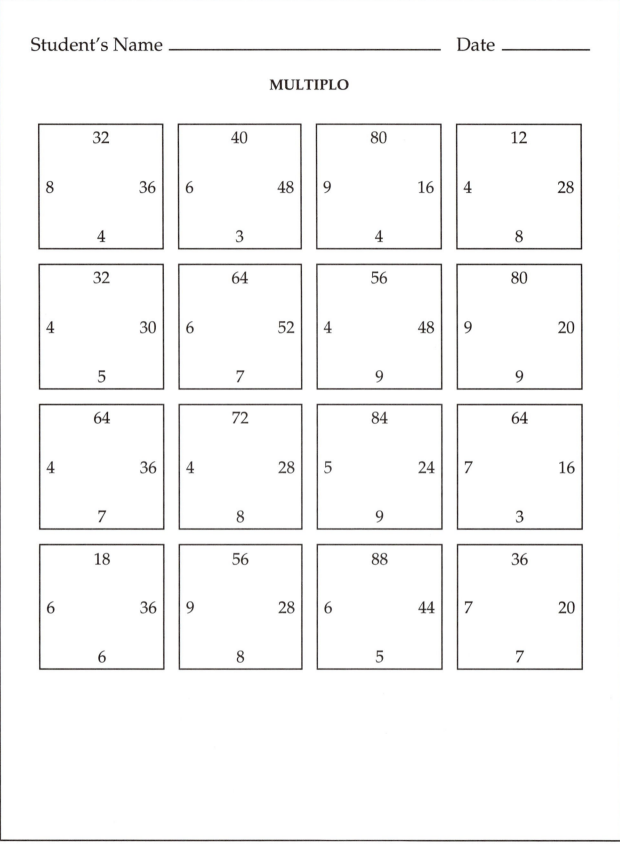

Student's Name _____ Date _____

FRACTION WHEEL

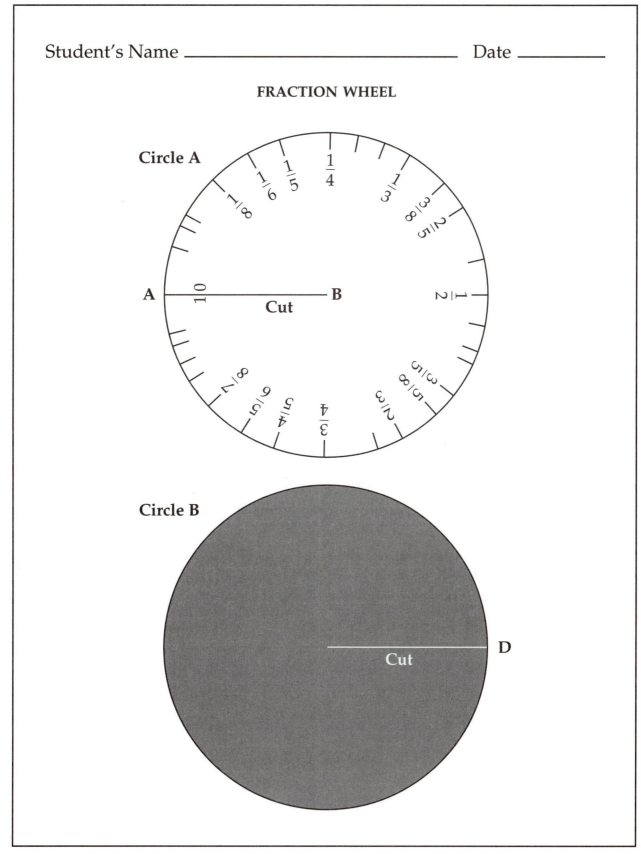

Circle A

Circle B

Student's Name _____ Date _____

TANGRAMS

Directions: Cut out the square below. Then carefully cut along the lines to separate the seven pieces of the tangrams.

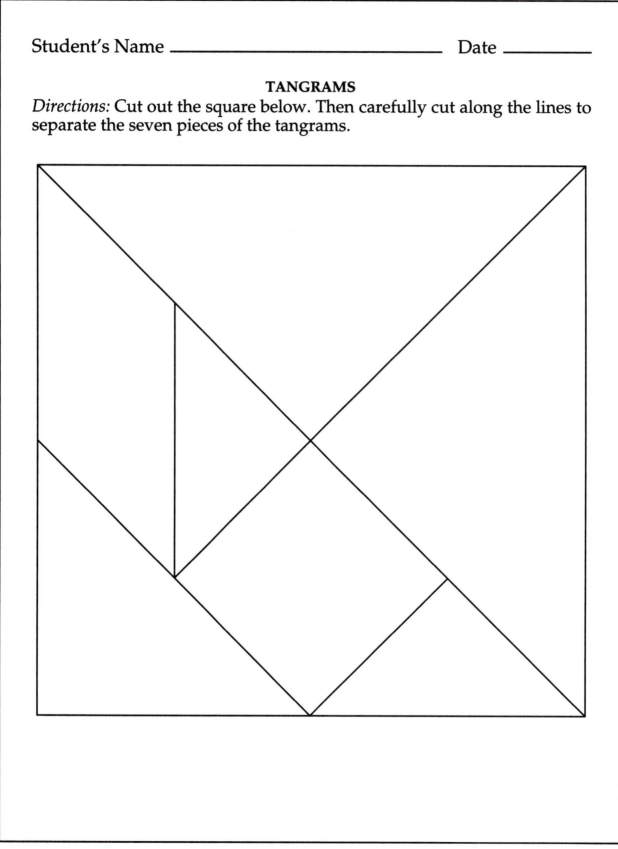

Student's Name _____ Date _____

FRACTION MAGIC SQUARES

Directions: In each of the following, you are able to complete the magic square and state the magic sum. In a magic square, each row, column, and diagonal must add up to the same sum. That sum is the magic sum.

	$2\frac{1}{16}$	
$2\frac{1}{3}$	$2\frac{7}{18}$	$2\frac{1}{9}$

Magic sum = _____

1		
	$2\frac{1}{2}$	
2		4

Magic sum = _____

$1\frac{1}{3}$		$2\frac{2}{3}$
		2

Magic sum = ___5___

$\frac{2}{5}$		$1\frac{1}{5}$
	$1\frac{1}{2}$	
$1\frac{4}{5}$		

Magic sum = _____

REPRODUCTION PAGE 19

Student's Name _____ Date _____

PLAYING MAT FOR MAKE A PROPORTION

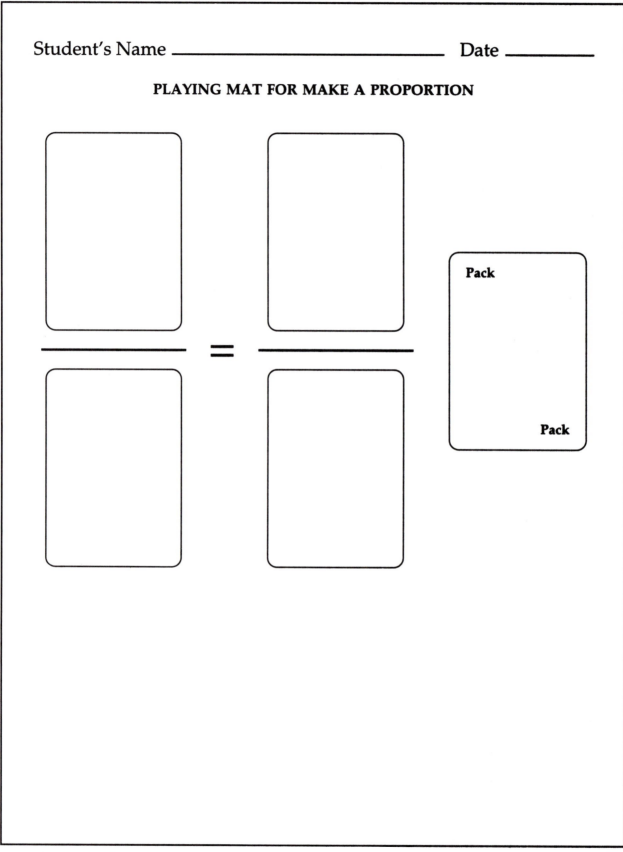

Student's Name _____ Date _____

GAME BOARDS FOR ROLLING FRACTIONS

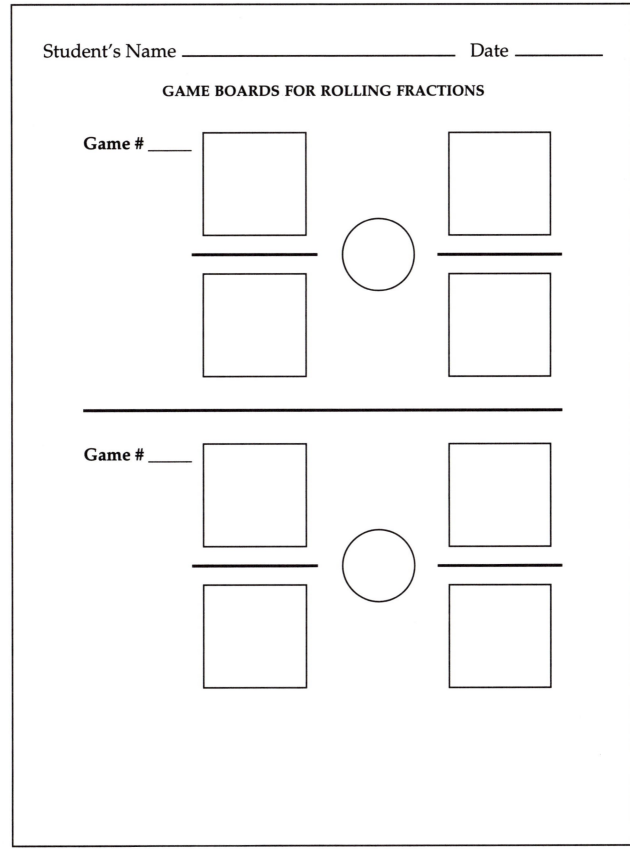

Game # _____

Game # _____

Student's Name _____ Date _____

GAME BOARDS FOR DECIMO

Game #1

Game #2

Game #3

Student's Name _____ Date _____

DECIMAL TIC-TAC-TOE GAME BOARD

Student's Name _____ Date _____

DECIMAL SHAPE DRILL

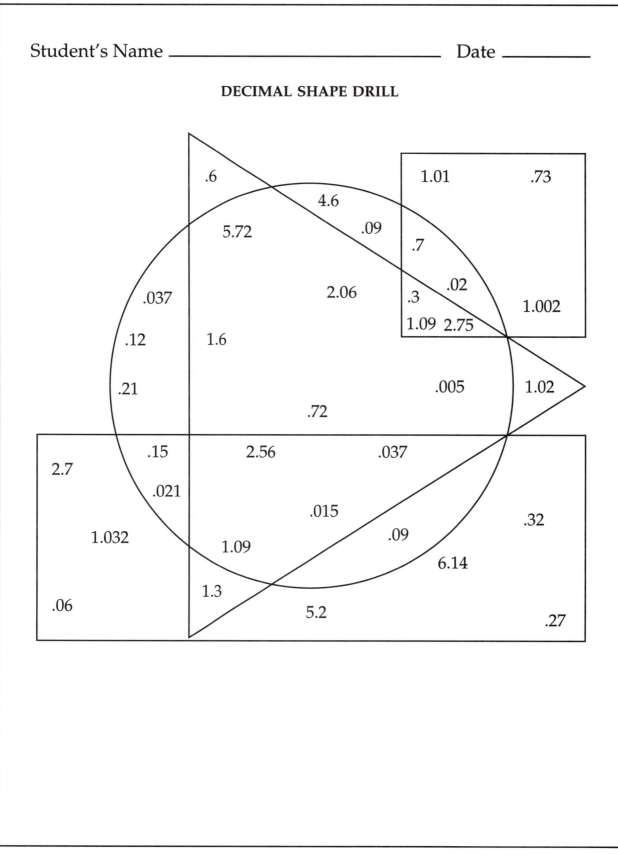

Student's Name ——————————————————— Date —————

DECIMAL SHAPE DRILL

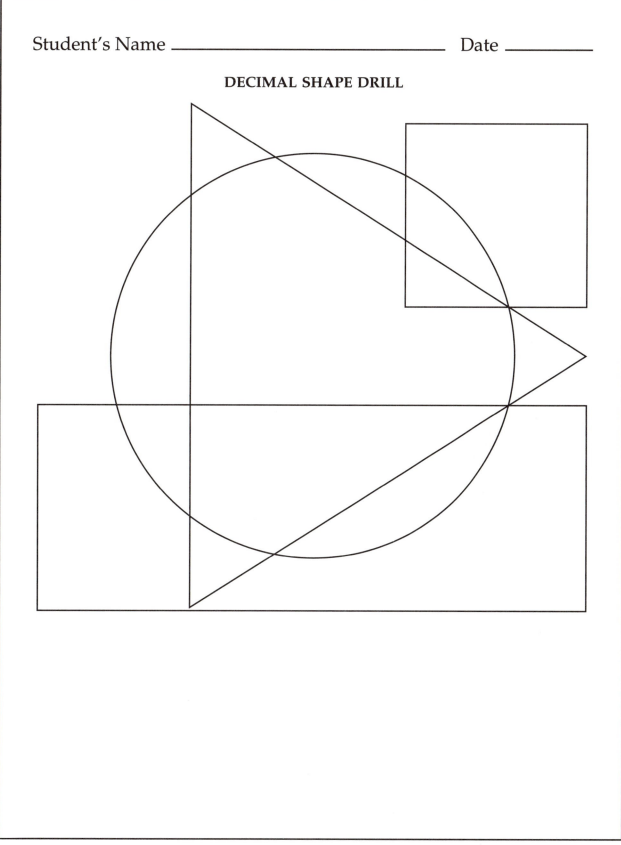

REPRODUCTION PAGE 25

Student's Name _____ Date _____

PERCENT COMPUTER

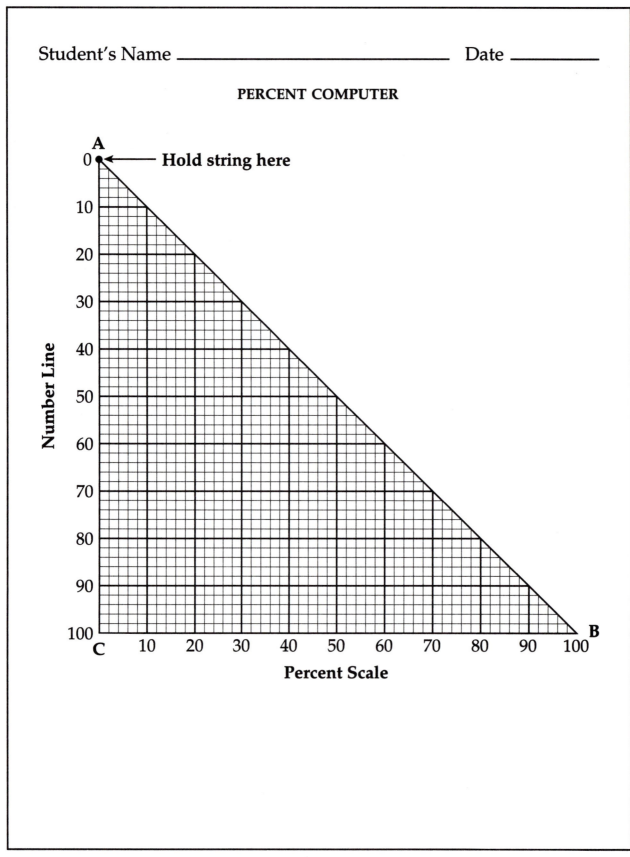

REPRODUCTION PAGE 26

Student's Name _____ Date _____

STRAWS AND TRIANGLES

Directions: You have been given five straws whose lengths are (a) 1", (b) 1½", (c) 2", (d) 2½" and (e) 3". Select any three pieces and attempt to form a triangle. Record the lengths and your results in the table. Two entries have already been done for you.

Pieces	Lengths			Can a Triangle Be Formed?
	Side 1	*Side 2*	*Side 3*	
a, b, c	1"	1½"	2"	Yes
a, b, d	1"	1½"	2½"	No

Answer the following questions:

How many different combinations did you try? _____

How many combinations did form a triangle? _____
How many did not? _____

What conclusions can you reach about the lengths of the sides of a triangle?

Student's Name _____ Date _____

SUM OF THE INTERIOR ANGLES OF A CONVEX POLYGON

Number of Sides	Number of Diagonals	Number of Triangles	Sum of the Interior Angles (Number of Triangles × 180°)
3	0	1	$1 \times 180° = 180°$
4	1	2	$2 \times 180° = 360°$
5	2	3	$3 \times 180° = 540°$
6			
7			
8			
n			

Student's Name _____ Date _____

RHOMBUS TILES

Student's Name _____ Date _____

TANGRAMS

Directions: Cut out the square shown below. Then carefully cut along the lines to create a seven-piece set of tangrams.

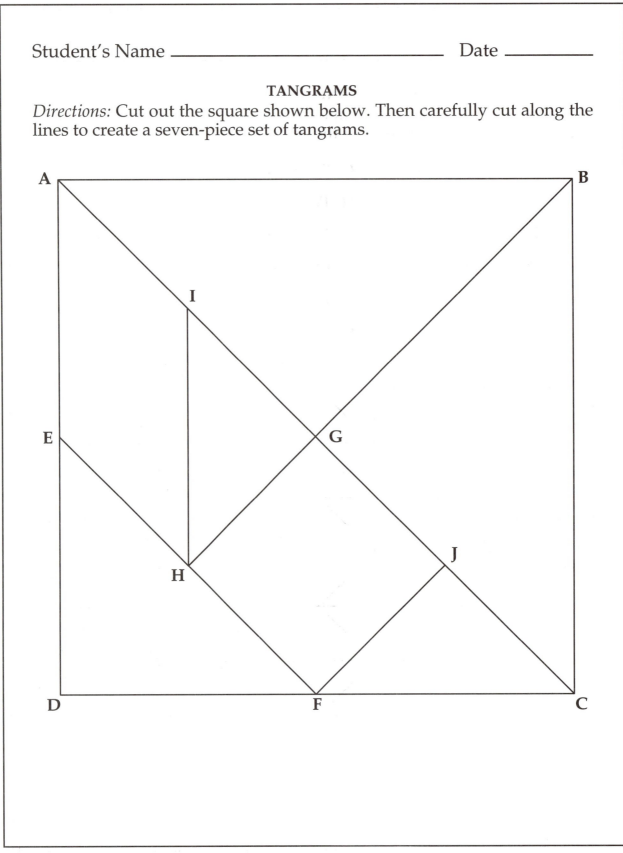

REPRODUCTION PAGE 30

Student's Name _____ Date _____

FIND ME!

Directions: Find as many of the shapes listed as you can. Shade in the shape on the grid and place the letter of the figure inside it.

A. Isosceles triangle   **G.** Trapezoid

B. Right triangle   **H.** Pentagon

C. Scalene triangle   **I.** Nexagon

D. Quadrilateral   **J.** Octagon

E. Rectangle   **K.** Rhombus

F. Parallelogram   **L.** Square

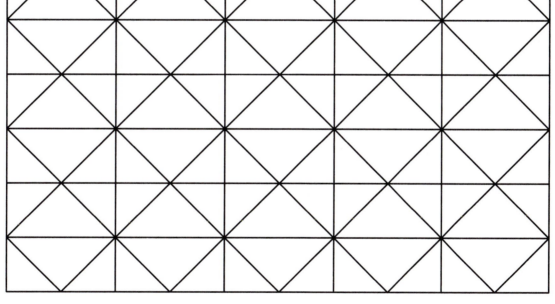

Student's Name _____ Date _____

A SET OF GEOMINOS

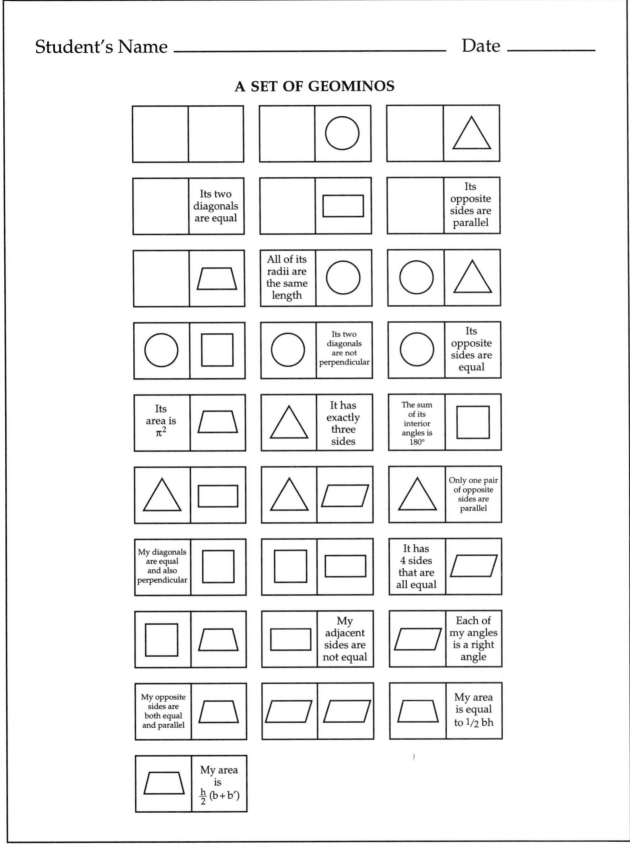

Student's Name _____ Date _____

GEOMETRY CONCENTRATION

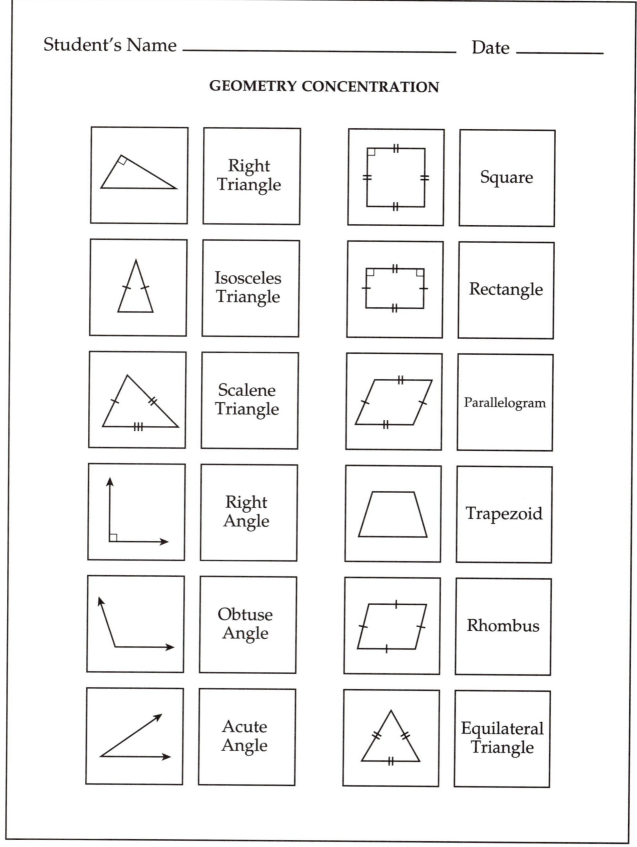

	Right Triangle
	Isosceles Triangle
	Scalene Triangle
	Right Angle
	Obtuse Angle
	Acute Angle
	Square
	Rectangle
	Parallelogram
	Trapezoid
	Rhombus
	Equilateral Triangle

Student's Name ——————————————— Date ———————

BOARD FOR APPROXIMATING PI

2 cm

Student's Name ————————————————— Date —————

AREA OF A CIRCLE

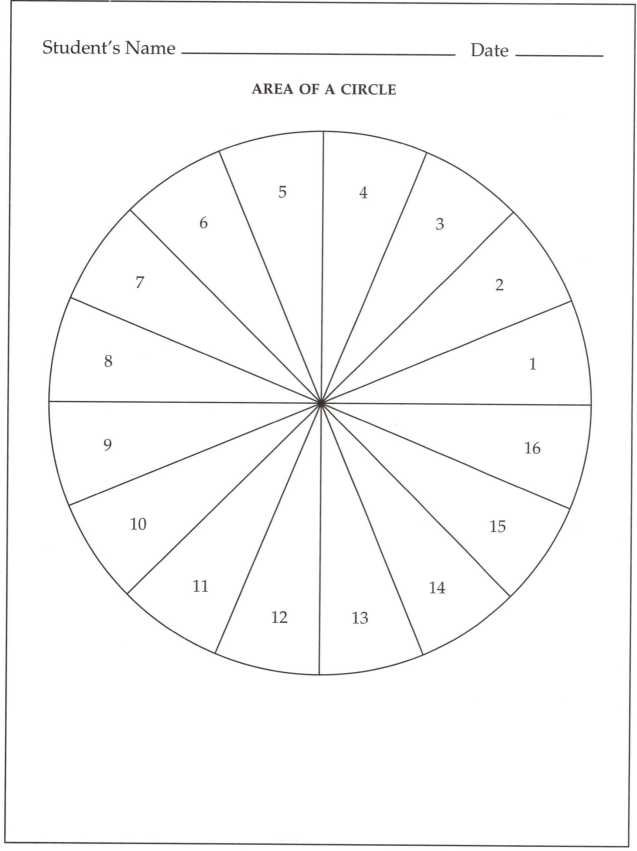

REPRODUCTION PAGE 35

Student's Name _____ Date _____

PENTOMINOES

Student's Name ——————————————————— Date ——————

MODEL FOR THE REGULAR TETRAHEDRON

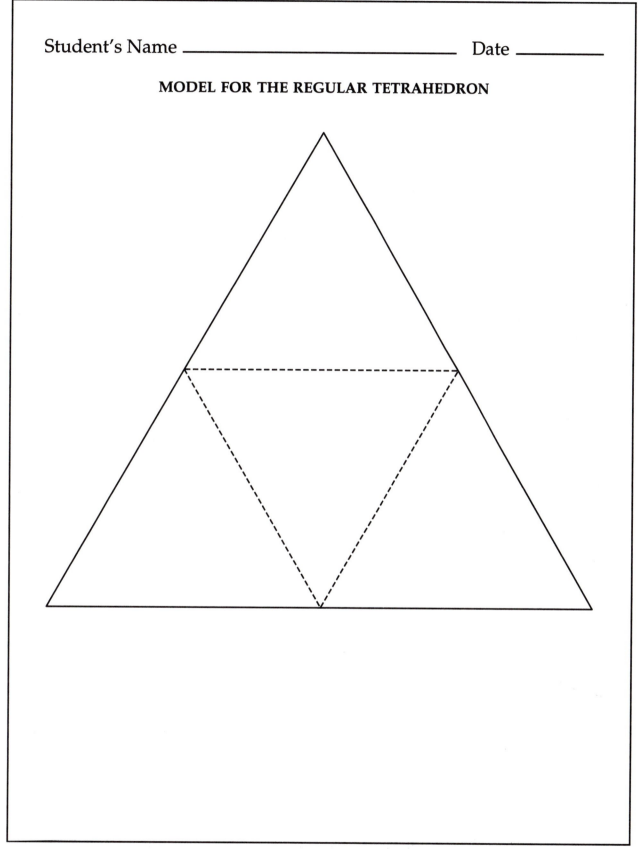

Student's Name ——————————————— Date ———————

MODEL FOR THE REGULAR HEXAHEDRON (CUBE)

Student's Name ———————————————————— Date ————————

MODEL FOR THE REGULAR OCTAHEDRON

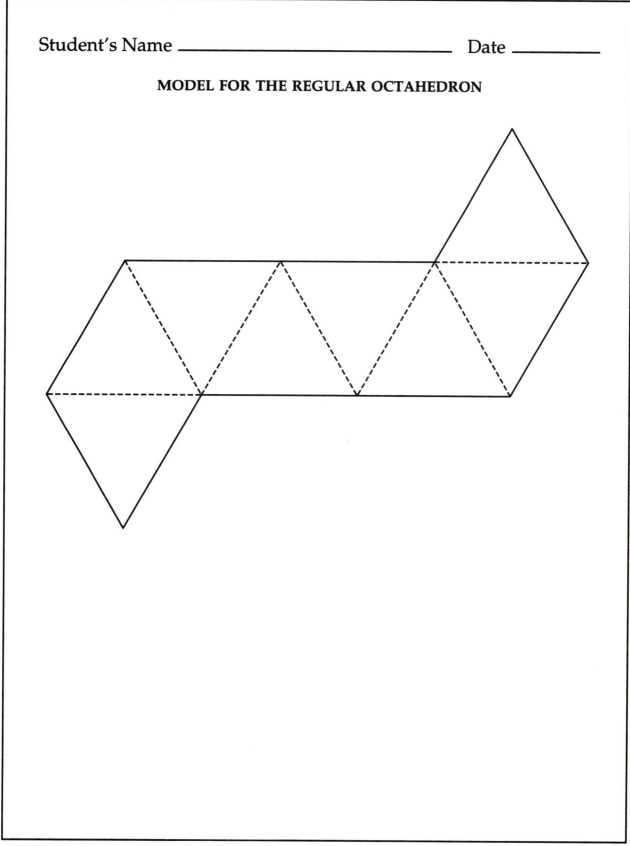

Student's Name ———————————————————— Date —————

MODEL FOR THE REGULAR DODECAHEDRON

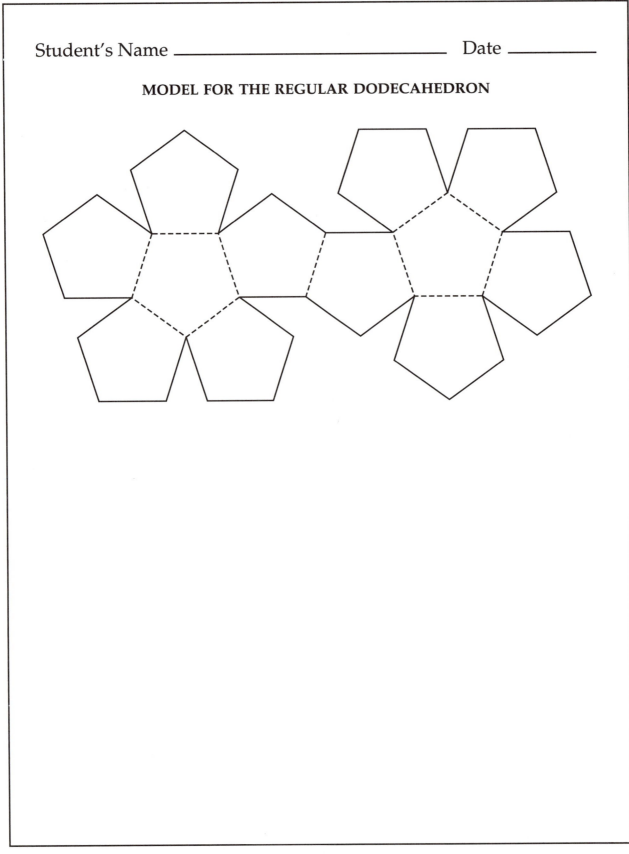

Student's Name ————————————————— Date ——————

MODEL FOR THE REGULAR ICOSAHEDRON

Student's Name _____ Date _____

BATTLESHIP GRID AND SHOT GRID

My Battleship Grid

9								
8								
7								
6								
5								
4								
3								
2								
1								
	A	B	C	D	E	F	G	H

My Shot Grid

9								
8								
7								
6								
5								
4								
3								
2								
1								
	A	B	C	D	E	F	G	H

Student's Name _____ Date _____

IT ALL ADDS UP!

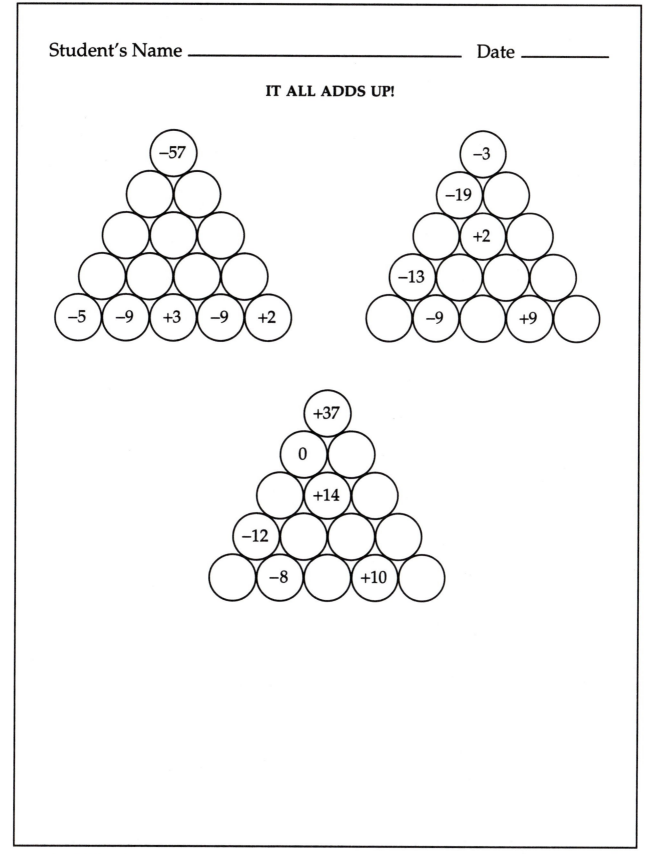

Student's Name _____ Date _____

INTEGER RACETRACK SPINNER

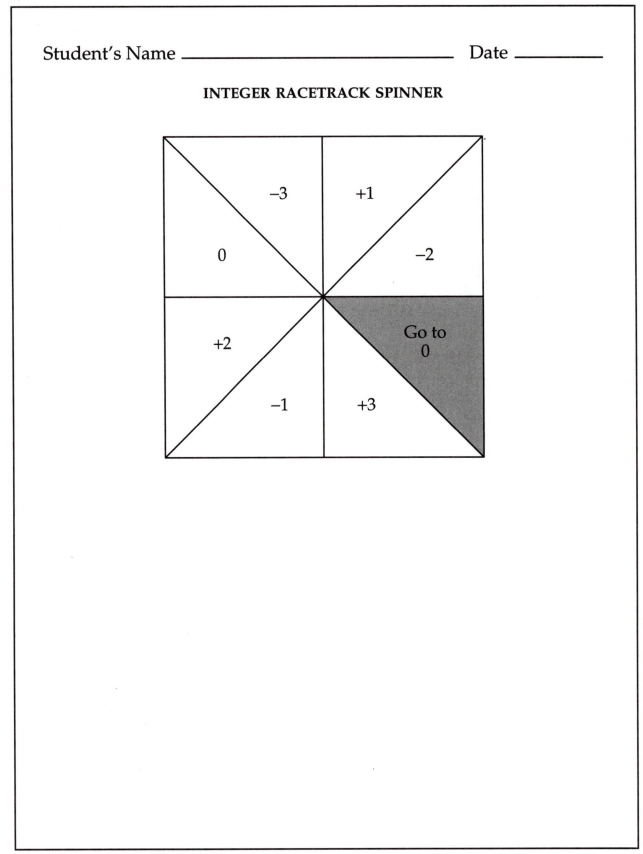

REPRODUCTION PAGE 44

Student's Name _____ Date _____

ALGEBRA TIC-TAC-TOE GAME BOARDS

Board #1

Board #2

Student's Name _____ Date _____

GAME BOARD FOR THE PEG GAME

Student's Name _____ Date _____

WHAT DOES THE MEAN REALLY MEAN?

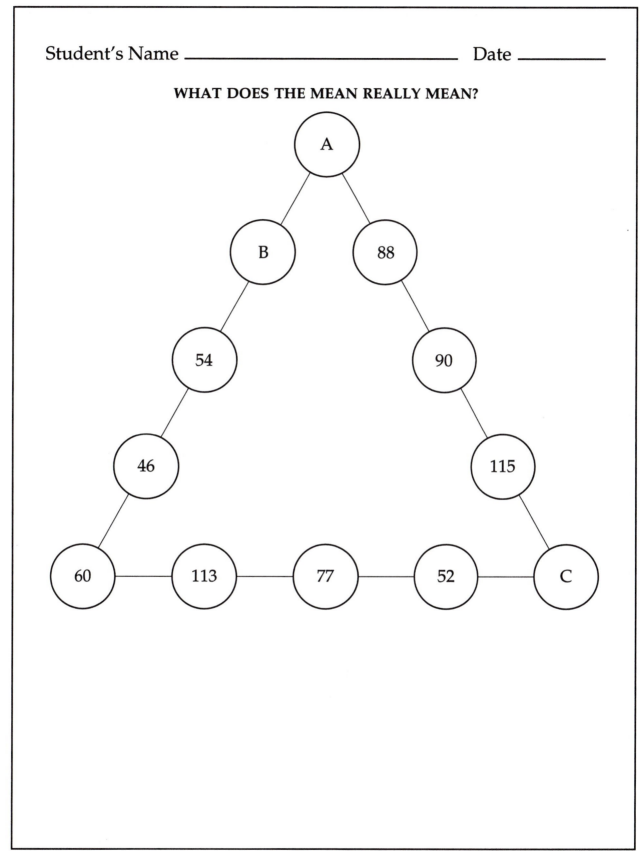

REPRODUCTION PAGE 47

Student's Name _____ Date _____

TABLE FOR "HOW FAR WILL IT ROLL?" DATA

Trial #	Height of Tube Top	Angle Tube Makes with the Floor	Distance Marble Rolls Before Stopping
1			
2			
3			
4			
5			
6			
7			
8			
9			
10			

Conclusions:

Height for maximum distance: _____

Angle for maximum distance: _____

REPRODUCTION PAGE 48

Student's Name _____ Date _____

"WHAT LETTER SHOULD WE PICK?" TALLY SHEET
Directions: Place a tally mark for each letter as it occurs in your paragraph.

A _____	N _____
B _____	O _____
C _____	P _____
D _____	Q _____
E _____	R _____
F _____	S _____
G _____	T _____
H _____	U _____
I _____	V _____
J _____	W _____
K _____	X _____
L _____	Y _____
M _____	Z _____

Student's Name _____ Date _____

MAYBE YES, MAYBE NO

Directions: Sometimes you can tell for sure that an event will or will not take place. Other times, you cannot be certain but know it probably will or probably will not. For each of the events described below, place a check in the appropriate column.

Event	Certainly Will	Certainly Will Not	Probably Will	Probably Will Not
1. It will rain sometime this month in your town.				
2. You will lose a tooth this month.				
3. You can roll a 7 with a single-number cube.				
4. In an auditorium with 375 people, at least 2 will have a birthday on the same day.				
5. New Year's Day will occur on February 3.				
6. When you toss a fair coin, it will land "tails up."				
7. In your class, there will be more girls than boys present on Tuesday.				

Event	Certainly Will	Certainly Will Not	Probably Will	Probably Will Not
8. The first car you see on the street will have your state's license plate.				
9. There are 15 slips of paper placed in a bag. Each has a number 1 through 15 written on it. You pick one at random. It has a prime number on it.				

Student's Name _____ Date _____

HOW MANY IN THE ENVELOPE?

Directions: In your envelope are 40 chips, some red, some blue, and some green. Shake the envelope. Without looking, draw a sample of 5 chips. Record the number of each color in the table below. Replace the chips. Shake and draw again. Do this a total of four times.

Trial	Red	Blue	Green
1			
2			
3			
4			
Totals			

1. Express your results as a fraction with a denominator of 20. _____

2. On the basis of your findings, how many of each color do your predict are in the envelope?   Red ____   Blue _____   Green _____

3. Explain how you made your prediction.

   _____

   _____

   _____

   _____

   You have conducted an experiment to determine *experimental probability.*

4. Now count the actual number of each color chip that is in your group's envelope.   Red ____   Blue _____   Green _____

5. Express these as fractions:

   Red $\dfrac{}{40}$ Blue $\dfrac{}{40}$ Green $\dfrac{}{40}$

   These are referred to as *theoretical probability.*

6. How close were your predictions to the actual number of each color tiles?

_____

_____

7. Your actual numbers probably didn't match your original predictions. Why not? How might you change the experiment to make your predictions closer to the actual numbers?

_____

_____

_____

_____

REPRODUCTION PAGE 51

Student's Name _____ Date _____

"IAN'S DINOSAURS"

Ian wants to collect all six model dinosaurs that are being given away in boxes of his favorite breakfast cereal. Each box contains one of the models, and there is an equally likely chance of any one model being in any one box. The store has 600 boxes in stock, containing 100 of each model.

1. How many boxes of the cereal do you think Ian must buy to be certain that he has one of each model dinosaur? _____
2. How many boxes of the cereal do you think Ian should buy to be reasonably sure of having one of each model? _____

To answer question 2, you are going to perform an experiment using the mathematical idea of random numbers. Each roll of the die is a simulation of buying 1 box of cereal.

1. Each of the numbers from 1 to 6 will represent one of the model dinosaurs.
2. Roll the die and record the number you get. Continue to roll the die until you have rolled at least one of each of the numbers from 1 to 6.
3. Repeat this experiment a total of five times.
4. Combine the results your group obtained with those of the other groups in the class.
5. Now compute the average number of rolls it took the class to obatin one of each of the six numbers. This is the number of boxes of cereal that Ian should buy to be reasonably certain that he has at least one of each of the model dinosaurs.

REPRODUCTION PAGE 52

Student's Name _____ Date _____

"HOW GOOD IS YOUR GUESS?"

Here is a test for you to take. Unfortunately, someone lost the questions. But you can take the test anyway. Decide whether each question is True or False, and circle the correct choice.

1. T F	**6.** T F	**11.** T F	**16.** T F
2. T F	**7.** T F	**12.** T F	**17.** T F
3. T F	**8.** T F	**13.** T F	**18.** T F
4. T F	**9.** T F	**14.** T F	**19.** T F
5. T F	**10.** T F	**15.** T F	**20.** T F

a. What is the probability that you answered question 1 correctly? _____

b. What is the probability that you missed question 2? _____

c. What is the probability that the answer to question 3 is false? _____

d. The chances of each event above happening are based on theoretical probability. What do you think *theoretical probability* means? _____

_____

e. Your teacher will now read the correct answers for the 20 items above. Grade your own paper. What was your score? _____

Student's Name _____ Date _____

SQUARES FROM SQUARES

Column 1 *Trial*	Column 2 *Number Added*	Column 3 *Total Number of Tiles as a Sum*	Column 4 *Total Number of Tiles*
1	1	1	1
2	3	1 + 3	4
3	5	1 + 3 + 5	9
4			
5			
6			
n			

Student's Name _____ Date _____

CUBES FROM CUBES

Column 1 *Trial*	Column 2 *Number Added*	Column 3 *Total Number of Cubes as a Sum*	Column 4 *Total Number of Cubes*
1	1	1	1
2	7	1 + 7	8
3	19	1 + 7 + 19	27
4			
5			
6			
7			

Student's Name _____ Date _____

INTERSECTIONS

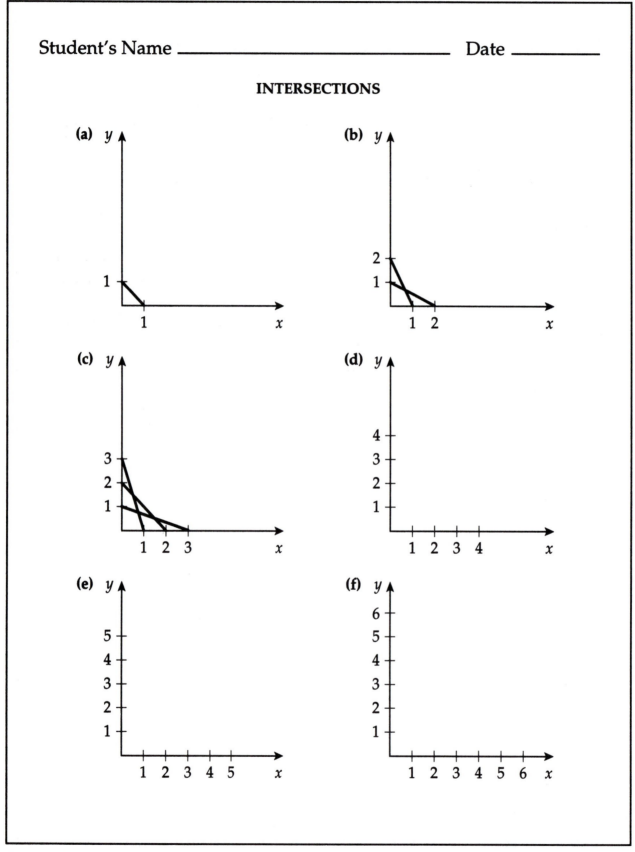

(a)

(b)

(c)

(d)

(e)

(f)

REPRODUCTION PAGE 56

Student's Name _____ Date _____

CODED MESSAGES

Directions: Answer the question below. Find the correct place to put each letter. Write the letter above the spot on the ruler. The first one is done for you.

What Will Happen to the Inchworm When We "Go Metric"?

U

U	11.5 cm	R	105 mm	G	12 cm
A	75 mm	C	50 mm	M	6 cm
B	4 cm; 11 cm	E	4.5 cm; 6.5 cm; 100 mm		
I	1 cm; 90 mm	L	25 mm; 3 cm; 85 mm		
'	2 cm	T	15 mm; 9.5 cm	O	5.5 cm

REPRODUCTION PAGE 57

Student's Name _____ Date _____

CAN YOU SOLVE THESE "EQUATIONS"?

Directions: In each of the following, supply the words that make each statement true. For example, number 1 is "6 = <u>S</u>ides in a <u>H</u>exagon."

1. 6 = S. in a H.
2. 360 = D. in a C.
3. 2000 = P. in a T.
4. 9 = I. in a B. G.
5. 212 = D. at which W. B.
6. 36 = I. in a Y.
7. 180 = D. in the A. of a T.
8. 1000 = G. in a K.
9. 4 = Q. in a G.
10. 365 = D. in a Y.

1. <u>Sides in a Hexagon</u>
2. _____
3. _____
4. _____
5. _____
6. _____
7. _____
8. _____
9. _____
10. _____

REPRODUCTION PAGE 58

Student's Name _____ Date _____

MATHEMATICAL WORD SEARCH

Directions: The following 21 mathematical terms can be found in the array of letters below. The words may be found horizontally, vertically, diagonally, forward, or backward. Put a circle around each word you find.

Arc	Congruent	Line	Pentagon	Set
Angle	Data	Mean	Perimeter	Similar
Area	Geometry	Median	Radius	Square
Base	Leg	Mode	Rectangle	Triangle
Chord				

```
E   N   I   L   O   L   E   G   M   T   P
R   E   S   A   B   N   L   E   S   C   E
S   P   E   N   T   A   G   O   N   O   N
Q   S   E   A   A   I   N   M   Z   N   S
U   E   M   R   P   D   A   E   C   G   I
A   T   E   B   I   E   T   T   H   R   M
R   A   M   R   A   M   C   R   O   U   I
E   M   O   E   T   S   E   Y   R   E   L
E   L   G   N   A   I   R   T   D   N   A
I   A   R   C   D   N   F   O   E   T   R
R   A   D   I   U   S   M   E   C   R   G
```

Student's Name _____ Date _____

METRIC WORD SEARCH

Directions: Find as many words and abbreviations dealing with metric measure as you can. Words may be found horizontally, vertically, diagonally, forward, or backward. Put a circle around each word or abbreviation you find.

```
K   M   M   I   L   L   I   M   E   T   E   R
I   A   R   E   A   J   A   C   C   M   E   E
L   E   N   G   T   H   S   I   U   M   I   T
O   R   C   H   R   R   R   B   E   B   S   I
T   U   I   E   A   A   I   T   D   M   E   L
C   L   T   M   L   N   E   C   E   N   T   I
H   E   O   U   A   R   A   S   C   A   L   E
M   R   N   H   K   L   S   L   I   N   E   H
M   A   N   O   T   M   A   R   G   R   T   M
E   A   E   V   H   D   C   T   A   D   E   B
R   I   Y   T   I   C   A   P   I   C   A   E
S   Q   U   A   R   E   N   W   I   D   T   H
```

Student's Name _____ Date _____

TABLES FOR WORD VALUE

Table 1

A = $1	G = $7	M = $13	S = $19	Y = $25
B = $2	H = $8	N = $14	T = $20	Z = $26
C = $3	I = $9	O = $15	U = $21	
D = $4	J = $10	P = $16	V = $22	
E = $5	K = $11	Q = $17	W = $23	
F = $6	L = $12	R = $18	X = $24	

Table 2

A = 50¢	G = $3.50	M = $6.50	S = $9.50	Y = $12.50
B = $1.00	H = $4.00	N = $7.00	T = $10.00	Z = $13.00
C = $1.50	I = $4.50	O = $7.50	U = $10.50	
D = $2.00	J = $5.00	P = $8.00	V = $11.00	
E = $2.50	K = $5.50	Q = $8.50	W = $11.50	
F = $3.00	L = $6.00	R = $9.00	X = $12.00	

Table 3

A = $4.00	G = $3.10	M = $2.20	S = $1.30	Y = .30
B = $3.85	H = $2.95	N = $2.05	T = $1.15	Z = .15
C = $3.70	I = $2.80	O = $1.90	U = $1.00	
D = $3.55	J = $2.65	P = $1.75	V = .75	
E = $3.40	K = $2.50	Q = $1.60	W = .60	
F = $3.25	L = $2.35	R = $1.45	X = .45	

REPRODUCTION PAGE 61

Student's Name _____ Date _____

WHICH DOESN'T BELONG AND WHY?

Directions: In each of the following 15 sets, you are to select the one item which you feel is different from the rest. Be prepared to give your reason for the choice you've made. More than one answer is possible.

1.	18	9	20	72
2.	$\sqrt{4}$	$\sqrt{7}$	$\sqrt{9}$	$\sqrt{16}$
3.	Tennis	Baseball	Hockey	Golf
4.	15	9	225	49
5.	Red	Orange	Yellow	Blue
6.	Rectangle	Pentagon	Trapezoid	Rhombus
7.	4334	8106	1991	747
8.	A	V	X	D
9.	1	8	81	1000
10.	16→24	100→150	40→60	33→36
11.	1776	1492	1931	1812
12.	New York	Atlanta	Harrisburg	Sacramento
13.	1 yard 4 inches	40 inches	2 feet 10 inches	3 feet 4 inches
14.	3	17	37	57
15.	New Jersey	New Mexico	New York	New England

Copyright © 2000 by Allyn and Bacon.

274

REPRODUCTION PAGE 62

Student's Name _____ Date _____

MIND-READING CARDS

Card I

1	3	5	7	9	11	13	15	17	19	21
23	25	27	29	31	33	35	37	39	41	43
45	47	49	51	53	55	57	59	61	63	

Card II

2	3	6	7	10	11	14	15	18	19	22
23	26	27	30	31	34	35	38	39	42	43
46	47	50	51	54	55	58	59	62	63	

Card III

4	5	6	7	12	13	14	15	20	21	22
23	28	29	30	31	36	37	38	39	44	45
46	47	52	53	54	55	60	61	62	63	

Card IV

8	9	10	11	12	13	14	15	24	25	26
27	28	29	30	31	40	41	42	43	44	45
46	47	56	57	58	59	60	61	62	63	

Card V

16	17	18	19	20	21	22	23	24	25	26
27	28	29	30	31	48	49	50	51	52	53
54	55	56	57	58	59	60	61	62	63	

Card VI

32	33	34	35	36	37	38	39	40	41	42
43	44	45	46	47	48	49	50	51	52	53
54	55	56	57	58	59	60	61	62	63	

Student's Name _____ Date _____

GOLDEN RATIOS

Directions—Part 1: Your group has been given a series of rectangles with which to work. You are to measure the length and width of each rectangle, compute the ratio of length/width in decimal form, and enter the data in the table below.

Object	Length	Width	L/W	Decimal
Index Card	5"	3"	1.67	

Part 2:

1. Compare the length of your arm and the distance from the finger tip of your middle finger to your elbow. Calculate the ratio. _____

2. Compare the length of your index finger and the distance from this fingertip to the large knuckle. Calculate the ratio. _____

3. How do your ratios compare to those of the other members of your group?

4. Find other objects that approximate the Golden Ratio.

Student's Name ——————————————— Date ————

THE SEVEN BRIDGES OF KOENIGSBERG

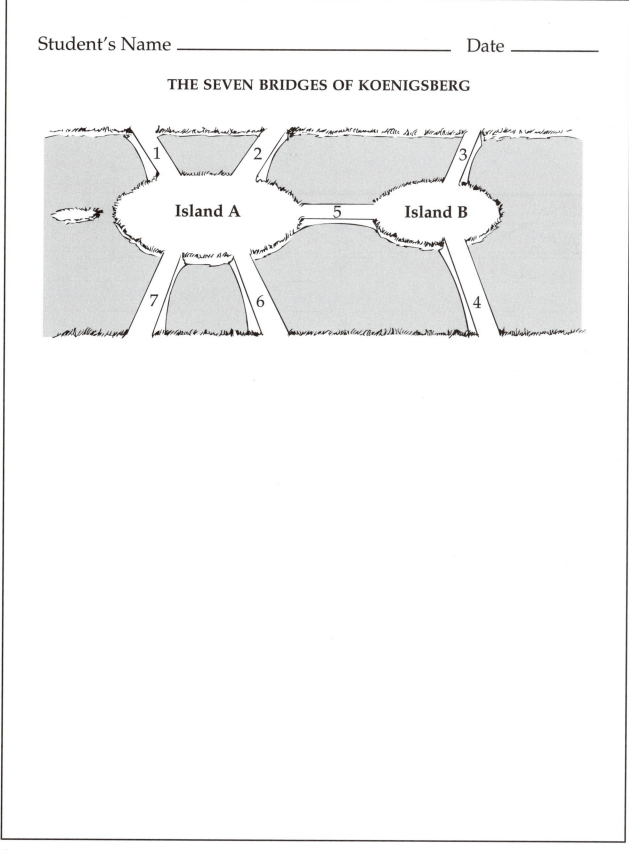

Student's Name _____ Date _____

SEVEN NETWORKS FOR THE KOENIGSBERG BRIDGES ACTIVITY

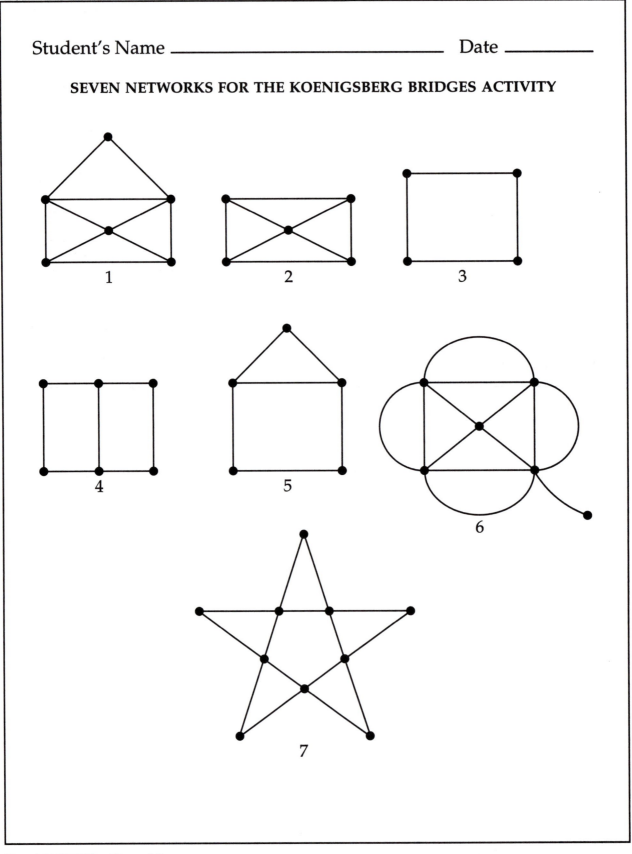

Student's Name ⎯⎯⎯⎯⎯⎯⎯⎯⎯⎯⎯⎯⎯ Date ⎯⎯⎯⎯⎯

DATA SHEET FOR THE KOENIGSBERG BRIDGES ACTIVITY

Network	Number of EVEN Vertices	Number of ODD Vertices	Can It Be Traced in One Continuous Line?
1			
2			
3			
4			
5			
6			
7			

Student's Name ——————————————————— Date ————————

SAMPLE MAPS FOR COLORING

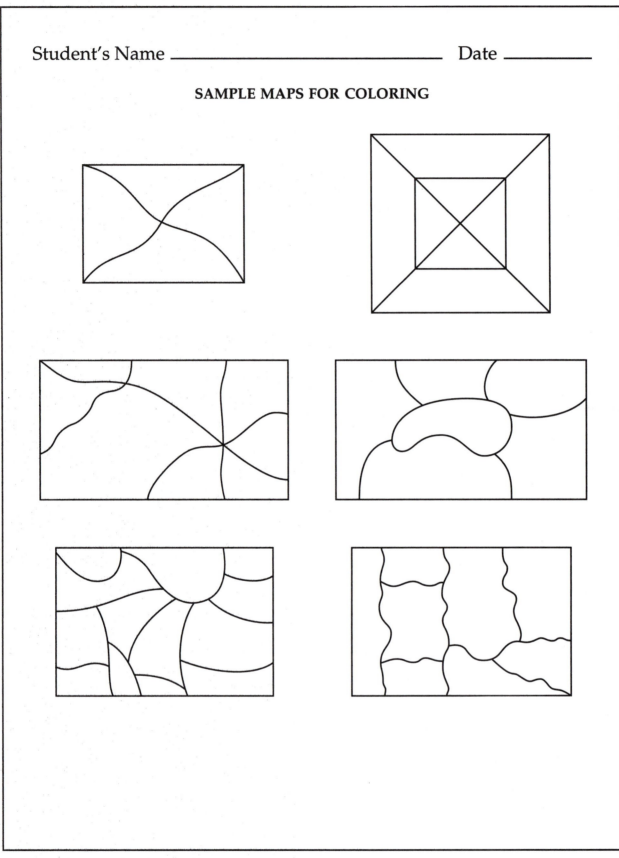

INDEX

Table of **Contents**